BILLY GLADSTONE

by Chet Falzerano

design and production by Jim Filippi

Pictured on the cover is a photo of William David "Billy" Gladstone that appeared on the August 1938 *The Metronome* magazine. It depicts Billy Gladstone superimposed over the Radio City Music Hall stage with the Radio City Music Hall Orchestra at the bottom. Through digital processing, the Gretsch-Gladstone snare pictured above was replaced with another Gretsch-Gladstone also owned by Billy Gladstone and later Ted Reed (see page 35).

TABLE OF CONTENTS

Dedication..4

Acknowledgements...5

Introduction..6

Billy Gladstone story..7

Gladstone Gallery color pages..73

This book is dedicated to my three sons

Nick, Jason and Chuck

and the memory of Liam Mulholland

Acknowledgments

My heartfelt thanks to:

William David "Billy" Gladstone, whose genius inspired this work

my publisher, Ron Middlebrook

my graphic artist, Jim Filippi and his magic computer

Tecno Style, Verbania Intra, Italy, for their technical support

Murray Spivack, Louie Bellson, Arthur Press, Eddie Jenkins, Bob Stuart, Duke Kramer,
Nick Fatool, Ted Reed, Phil Grant, Joe Morello, Jake Hanna, Frank Seigfired, Bill Hagner,
Elden C. "Buster" Bailey, Larry Bunker, Arnold Goldberg, Frankie Phelan, Eddie Caccavale,
Harold "Sticks" McDonald, Ken Ross, Glenn Robinson, Stanley Koor, Trudy Drummond Muegel,
Harry Sheppard, Herb Brochstein, and Morris "Arnie" Lang, for sharing with me
their personal experiences with Billy Gladstone

George A. Le Moine and Adrian Grad of Radio City Music Hall

Roger Turner, whose continuous support finally paid off

and John Aldridge, for his dedication to vintage drums

Introduction

If every unsung hero had his day in the sun it would be a bright day full of music. Though I would not consider Billy Gladstone an "unsung hero" (he was on the cover of *The Metronome* magazine) he deserves more attention for both his musical and inventive contributions. I first became aware of Billy Gladstone in the early eighties and have since been trying to quench my insatiable thirst for both knowledge and artifacts of this sensational musician/inventor. Herein is my account of this man with hopes that this will unearth more information about his prolific and colorful life.

Chet Falzerano

BILLY GLADSTONE

"My roll is probably the best roll in the world outside of one other drummer and I'm not modest. The greatest drummer that I have heard in my life as far as rudiments and the roll is concerned is Billy Gladstone".[1]

If you haven't guessed, the author of this quote was Buddy Rich (Mr. Modest), arguably accepted as the best drummer in the history of skin beaters. Praise from this master (seldom bestowed) is indeed an acknowledgment of Billy Gladstone's prowess on the snare drum. Buddy Rich was not alone in his opinion. In the October 1981 *Modern Drummer* article "Billy Remembered" Louie Bellson is quoted "I can recall one time going to hear Billy at Radio City (Music Hall in New York City) and he did something I never saw a drummer do and probably will never see again. The Rockettes were onstage, when suddenly Billy did one of those great sforzando rolls that was so magnificent that the attention of the entire theatre audience was literally drawn from the stage over to Billy's corner of the orchestra pit. Something like that happens once in a hundred years and it demon-

strates the kind of drumming magic this guy had. He was the epitome of a snare drum player. I only wish the kids of today had a chance to hear Billy Gladstone play". That same article quotes Joe Morello with "He (Gladstone) could do single stroke rolls at an incredible speed, and stay relaxed. Frankly, I've never heard a snare drummer who had the control and speed that Billy had". Barrett Deems

WILLIAM D. GLADSTONE

Distinguished Drummer and Inventor

Mr. Gladstone (his thousands of friends and admirers know him better as "Billy") is a featured favorite in Erno Rapee's superb Radio City Music Hall Symphony Orchestra where he has played drums ever since the opening of that famous New York theatre. Enjoying world-wide reputation as one of the outstanding drum-artists of our time, Billy Gladstone is an inventive genius as well, with 15 successful patents already to his credit. The GRETSCH-GLADSTONE DRUM features no less than three improvements of his invention—improvements born of his own practical experience and first-hand knowledge of drummers' needs—improvements of such vital and practical character that any one of them on a drum would serve to distinguish it above all others.

Billy Gladstone, Author's collection.

"Billy could play a roll that was so clean, it sounded like sand pouring out of a pitcher".[2]

---

[1] Taken from a recording submitted to the author by Ted Reed. This recording was made ca.1957 at a drummer's convention in Philadelphia

[2] "Billy Remembered" *Modern Drummer*, vol. 5 no. 7 Modern Drummer Publications, Inc., Cedar Grove, NJ, 1981

Gladstone's command of snare drum technique was not his only claim to fame. He was also a consummate inventor with more than 20 US patents credited to him. This duality inspired a July 1939 *Mechanix Illustrated* article "He Makes Money". Alan Finn writes, "Billy Gladstone, in the short space of a few

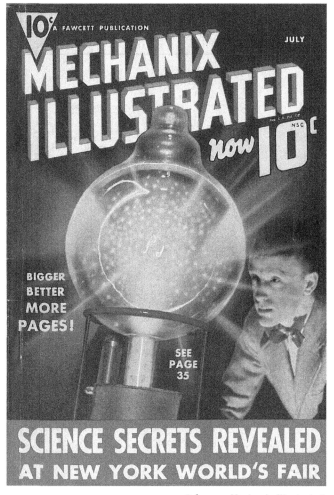

July 1939 *Mechanix Illustrated,*
Courtesy *Home Mechanix*, Times Mirror, formerly *Mechanix Illustrated*, Fawcett Publications .

years, has invented no fewer than 40 items. Being one of America's drum wizards, it is only natural that this inventor-musician has turned his inventive skill to musical lines. But his talent for all sorts of kitchen gadgets and other novelties is no less rich and productive".[3] From key cases to juice extractors to lighted tongue depressors, Gladstone's creative genius continued even after he left the bandstand.

Born December 15, 1892 in Rumania, William David Goldstein fell victim to an Ellis Island clerical error when he came to the United States in 1904. An officer referred to him as David Gladstone and the name stuck. "His father, an Englishman named Charles,was called by the Rumanian Government to supervise the Government Band that played for the entertainment of officers and officials. Billy, then about 7 years old was in the band for amusement value. He sat with his mouth on the mouthpiece of a big baritone horn which was filled with paper. He did not play a note but he made some grand flourishes, and one night the local Governor told him he was the best member of the band. A rise of ten pennies a month and a promotion to the rank of 'sergeant' gave the boy a rather exalted opinion of himself. The next night he took the paper out of the horn and tried to play. He did fairly well until the rest of the band paused and he released a sour note. The child, however, soon learned the instrument, and when in a few years after he came to New York he knew the rudiments of most brasses.

In his teens he got a job as a messenger boy at one of the city's great department stores (Wanamakers), largely because he had heard that the emporium had a staff drum and bugle corps and he thought he could combine business and music without difficulty. (He joined) up in the corps, applying for the post of bugler. What they really needed were drummers. So 'Billy' started drumming. It was the first time in his life that he'd held drumsticks in his hands, but he was so successful that he soon became a star in the corps. He's been a star at the drums ever since. As the years went by he found himself on Broadway, playing in theatre orchestras. But it was symphonic stuff that he wanted. Popular music and dance stuff had little appeal to him. So he was a happy drummer when he was hired to play in the first orchestra Erno Rapee was to conduct on the Great White Way. That was when the (later) Music Hall's music director introduced fine music to Broadway movie audiences over two decades long before the Radio City theatre opened its doors. (1932). And Gladstone has played under Mr. Rapee's direction ever since".[4]

Emo Rapee,
Courtesy Radio City Music Hall.

[3] "He Makes Money" by Alan Finn, *Mechanix Illustrated,* vol.12 no. 3 Fawcett Publications,Inc., Louisville, KY, 1939
[4] "His Inventions Run to Music" Radio City Music Hall Publicity Department, Rockefeller Center, New York, NY

Billy was the percussionist at the Capitol Theatre on Broadway under the baton of Erno Rapee when it opened in 1919. Major Edwin C. Bowes was the Managing Director and controlled the entire operation of the theatre. It was also about this time that Gladstone's inventive genius began to mushroom. On June 28, 1922, Billy, along with a colleague by the name of Emil Kun, applied for a patent (number 1,508,390) for a "Double Action Bass Drum Pedal".

Early Bass Drum Pedal equipped with a "Clanger". Author's collection.

wood, the action or speed of these pedals left much to be desired. It was William F. Ludwig, Sr. that manufactured the first mass produced bass drum pedal "To keep up with the new 'Rag Time' tempos". Ludwig's idea was pirated by various manufactures and all sorts of pedals were released to the market. Fortunately for Ludwig, his maiden offering was an immediate success resulting in a drum empire that continues to this day. Gladstone's concept took the foot pedal idea to a whole new realm. "Our invention relates to improvements in foot pedals to be used for playing bass-drums in orchestras or bands, in which strokes may be executed by the action of both the toe or heal of the

Actual "Double Action Bass Drum Pedal" patent owned by Billy Gladstone, Author's collection.

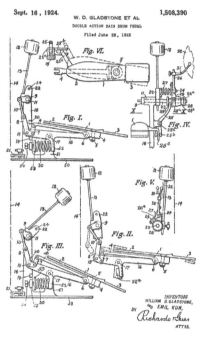

"Double Action Bass Drum Pedal" patent drawing, Author's collection.

Around the turn of the century for economic and spacial reasons, percussion sections consisting of one or more snare drummers, a bass drummer and cymbal player were consolidated into one person known at the time as "double drumming". Through necessity, drummers created pedals operated by the foot that would strike both the bass drum and a small cymbal mounted to the hoop of the bass drum. These pedals, however, were the bane of trap or drumset players. Often crude contraptions made of

foot; the object of our invention being to enable the performer to execute the fastest passages written for bass-drums with very little effort; second, to make it possible to change the length and therefore the strength (amplitude) of the stroke by simply increasing or decreasing the (downward) pressure of the foot on the pedal; and third, to enable the performer to make the cymbal-beater operative or inoperative in unison with the drumbeater by a slight rotation of his foot, without taking the same off the pedal. A further object is to provide an apparatus of this character in which the return movement of the beater is accomplished without the use of springs for this purpose and as a result thereof avoiding the necessity for the performer having to exert the force required to overcome the spring pressure, which obviously becomes quite fatiguing to the performer".[5] Clearly years ahead of its time, Gladstone's first patent, approved in 1924, though excellent and totally credible, was sadly never manufactured.

Gladstone had very definitive ideas on the inventing process. "For years I had thought up many little devices and mechanical improvements on things. I foolishly showed them to people. I suddenly woke up to find my ideas had been filched. My gadgets were being patented by others. A struggling inventor is up against a lot of problems. He ought to study the field thoroughly, just as he would going into any other work. It isn't merely a question of possessing an interesting idea. More important considerations are: Is it practical? Will it work? Can it be made at a small cost? Manufacturers are keen today

Gladstone seated at a piano with his patents as his score, Courtesy *Home Mechanix*, Times Mirror, formerly *Mechanix Illustrated,* Fawcett Publications.

for things which can fit in with their machinery, raw materials, and program. Simplicity is a great drawing card with them. It'll get a man on first base right away if he has something worthwhile. Take my key case (more later). It's just a round chain and a bit of leather with a couple of holes plugged in it. In fact, the manufacturer uses the leftover from wallet cuttings, which is a boon to him'.

When admirers survey Billy Gladstone's array of inventions the first question they usually ask is: How do you do it? His answer is simple. He studies the thing he wants to improve or create. He works it over and over in his mind until some tangible picture emerges. Sometimes the image crystallizes as he pounds away at the percussion instruments, sometimes as he deliriously dodges charging taxicabs along busy Fiftieth street while stage door attendants gasp in horror.

Whatever the case may be Billy gets as soon as possible to pad and pencil and scrawls his brain child down. Then he polishes the sketch until he's satisfied it's right, and takes it around to his patent attorney. Getting the proper advice is as important as creating the idea, he says. 'You can't be too careful, today', he explained. 'I always have copies of my final sketches notarized, dated, sealed with wax and mailed to myself. I do this before ever mentioning a word of the invention to anyone except my attorney'. But getting the patent and then a prospective manufacturer may not end the inventor's struggle, according to young Mr. Gladstone. 'Manufacturers are in business. Not frequently they have bought something similar to your device, but perhaps not as good. They'll sign a contract with you and put your invention on the shelf to rust. That's why I advise having a good attorney. Business is business. There is plenty of money if you hit the right inventions. But everything may depend on the connections you make. So watch out'".[6]

Gladstone's next patent (number 1,611,432) was granted in 1926 entitled "Support for Musical Instruments." Essentially a collapsible snare drum stand, it's obvious flimsy structure did not get the attention of drum companies and was also never manufactured. In 1927 he was granted a patent (number

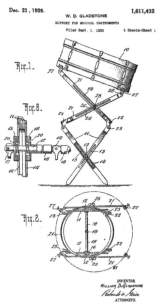

"Support For Musical Instruments" patent drawing, Author's collection.

5 "Double-Action Bass-Drum Pedals" United States Patent Office, no. 1,508,390, Washington, DC, 1924
6 "He Makes Money" by Alan Finn, *Mechanix Illustrated,* vol.12 no. 3 Fawcett Publications, Inc., Louisville, KY, 1939

1,621,777) for a "Key Holder", but the design was not well thought-out as his later version. This too, did not see the light of a new marketing day. Again in 1927 he was granted a patent (number 1,630,701) for a "Drum Support ing Device" or what drummers commonly refer to as "spurs" for the bass drum. This design was problematical, as the mounting structure would unwantedly affect the tuning of the drum. Gladstone: "It may sound strange, but some-times in my despair I was ready to tear up my patents. When my ideas didn't seem to interest a manufac-turer I just wanted to throw them in the wastebasket. But I never gave up, I kept plug-ging, trying".

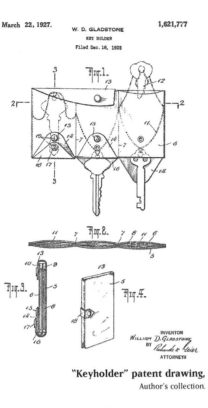

"Keyholder" patent drawing, Author's collection.

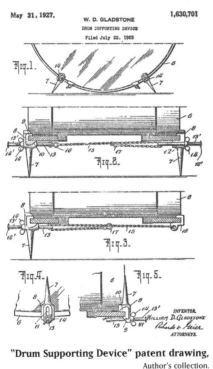

"Drum Supporting Device" patent drawing, Author's collection.

Gladstone's tenacity finally paid off later in 1927 when his patent (number 1,643,553) for an "Operating Device for Cymbals" caught the atten-tion of the Leedy Manufacturing Company, Inc. As noted before, early bass drum pedals included a second beater that struck a cymbal mounted on the bass drum hoop. "This ap-paratus was often called a 'clanger' - rightly so, since the resulting tone was a rather monotonous clanging sound. (Double) Drum-mers desiring the more pleasant sound of two cymbals played together first developed the snowshoe pedal. Its construction was simply two cymbals mounted between two foot-shaped boards with a spring hinge. The player slipped his foot into the toe strap (hence the term 'snowshoe') and could either execute a crash or 'chick' sound, depending on the attack". Various versions of the "low boy" or "sock cymbal" appeared on the market but it soon evolved to the hi hat, whereby the pair of cymbals were raised to a playable level with drumsticks. "Some drummers (at the time) were not certain the device should be foot operated. Many hand-held cymbals were also listed in early catalogues".[7] On page 42 of the 1928 Leedy cata-logue, three versions of the hand-held cymbals were offered: "Sting Cymbals, Squash Cymbals", and finally, Gladstone's first patent to be universally marketed by a prominent drum manufacturer, the "Hand Sock Cymbals". Leedy's de-scription, "One of the finest modern Drummer's effects and flashes ever presented. They can be made to pro-duce a world of varied effects

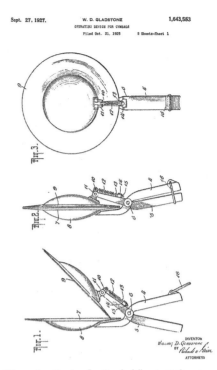

"Operating Device for Cymbals" patent drawing, Author's collection.

Leedy Hand Held Cymbals, Author's collection.

<hr>

[7] "The Evolution Of The Hi-Hat" by Chet Falzerano, *Modern Drummer*, vol. 14, no. 9 Modern Drummer Publications, Inc., Cedar Grove, NJ, 1990

in straight or syncopated rhythms. Will either 'ring' or 'sock'. Many Drummers use them in pairs, one in each hand, for solo work. Wonderful for breaks, etc. These cymbals were invented by Bill Gladstone of the Capitol Theatre, New York City". Item number 270 is price listed at $8.00 ($92.71 in 2006 dollars). Pictured along with 22 colleagues, "Bill" Gladstone appears on the inside back cover of the catalogue along with the editorial "A few 'big timers' who say (in one form or another) 'I play Leedy instruments because I think they are the

Joe Castka, colleague of Billy at Radio City Music hall playing two pair,
Courtesy *Home Mechanix*, Times Mirror, formerly *Mechanix Illustrated*, Fawcett Publications.

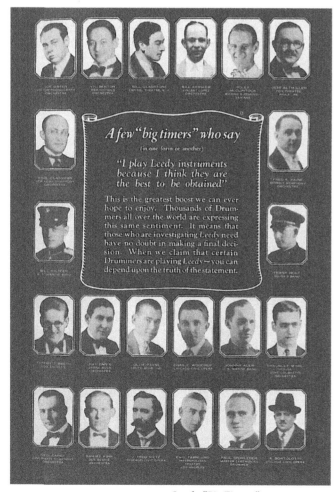

Leedy "Big Timers", Author's collection.

best to be obtained' [8]. Imagine Gladstone's sentiment at not only receiving industry recognition as a great performer (his first endorsement deal) but acknowledgment of his inventive genius as well. During the development process of the Hand Sock Cymbals, Billy sought out the opinion of a well-respected colleague. Murray Spivack was the staff drummer at the Arcadia Ball Room. "Bill Gladstone presented me with the (prototype) cymbals in 1927. His object in giving them to me was to find out whether they were loud enough to be heard through the dance band in the Arcadia Ball Room, which was the largest ball room in New York

Gladstone's prototype pair of Hand Sock Cymbals,
Author's collection.

City. They were loud enough and I did get to the point, after a bit of practice, (that) I was able to play some licks between (a stick in my right hand) and the sock cymbal (in my left). Bill and I were very good friends".

Spivack's admiration for Gladstone was also noted by Louie Bellson, "I first heard about Billy Gladstone while I was studying with Murray Spivack. Guys have always associated that finger technique with me

Murray Spivak at Arcadia Ball Room using prototype pair of hand sock cymbals,
Author's collection

because they've seen me do it. But actually, I got it from Murray and Billy Gladstone, who in turn got their concepts of finger technique from the French and Swiss drummers. But Murray always used to say that Billy was the real master and the leading exponent of the finger system". [9]

[8] Leedy Manufacturing Company Inc. catalogue "R", Indianapolis, IN, 1928
[9] "Billy Remembered" *Modern Drummer*, vol. 5 no. 7 Modern Drummer Publications, Inc.,Cedar Grove, NJ, 1981

An excellent reference for Bellson and Spivack's interpretation of finger technique can be seen on Warner Brothers Publications/CPP Media Group's video *MURRAY SPIVACK, A lesson with Louie Bellson*, VH0256. Produced by Sandy Feldstein, this loving tribute to a master musician and teacher also features David Garibaldi, another Spivack student. Bellson, "Few people know this, but he (Gladstone) was part of a quartet. Murray Spivack, Billy Gladstone, Max Manne, Shelly Manne's father, and Carl Glassman who played timpani with Toscanini, were known as 'The Four Horsemen' in New York. Whenever something had to be done to perfection in percussion, they hired one of those four guys, or maybe two or three of them, or all four". Another excellent demonstration of the Gladstone finger technique can be seen on Warner Brothers Publications/DCI Music Video *Legends of Jazz Drumming Part Two 1950-1970*, VHO249. Joe Morello, former student of Billy Gladstone, performs a classic drum solo in "Take Five"with the Dave Brubeck Quartet. Recorded during the CBS program *Look Up and Live* in 1959, Morello can be seen comping with his right hand while performing incredibly fast single strokes with his left. I asked Morello about the position of his left hand in this video. I noted that in Bellson's video, Louie had a palm up position with his left hand while Joe's left hand was more palm down. When I inquired as to which position Gladstone used, Morello responded "Both...it's a combination of utilizing the rebound of the drum and development of the wrist and fingers".

attention of Leedy. Shown in the first patent, but not included in the Leedy catalogue, was a floor stand, enabling the Hand Sock to be used also as a low boy. Gladstone's following two patents ("Percussion Musical Instrument"), granted in 1931 (number 1,801,422) and in 1932 (number 1,843,553) were for the xylophone. Both were dampening devices, the first mechanical, the second electrical.

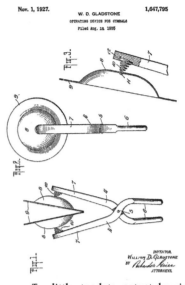

Too little. too late, patent drawing, Author's collection.

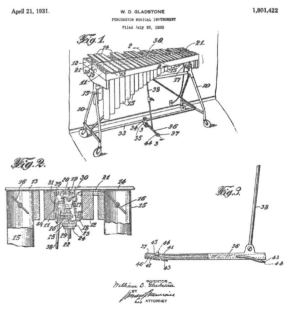

Gladstone's hand sock cymbal floor stand, Author's collection.

Prior to Leedy including Billy's Hand Sock Cymbals, he was granted a patent (number 1,647,795) late in 1927 for a simpli-

Chick Webb (right) and band, note Gladstone cymbals in Chick's hand, Author's collection.

fied version of the Operating Device for Cymbals. Maybe this was an attempt on his part to follow his own advice of "Simplicity is a great drawing card". Obviously this was not necessary, as his earlier version drew the

"Percussion Musical Instrument" patent drawing, Author's collection.

A rather youthful looking Gladstone is pictured in the January 1931 *Leedy Drum Topics*. Standing next to Conductor Bunchik, Ray Becraft, Bill Bitner and Ray Becher at the Capitol Theatre, the article reads ening the term "contraptions" for which drummers were responsible to create a particular sound. It is no wonder that the inventive mind of Billy Gladstone yielded a plethora of effects. Later, "In the pioneer

"Stars of the Capitol" January 1931 *Leedy Drum Topics*, Author's collection.

"Each one of the drummers is an artist in the particular position which he fills and we do not believe that there are any better drummers in the country today than this all star outfit". Billy is then singled out "Bill Gladstone, the pit drummer, is a particularly talented performer and probably without peer in the United States or anywhere else in the world today. Those who are familiar with Bill's work know him to be one of the profession's outstanding examples of extraordinary ability, not only as a performer on Drum, Tympani, and Xylophone, but also as an authority on the technicalities of drummers' instruments and an expert on sound effects".[10]

During the silent movie days (pre 1927), drummers in the orchestra pits of movie theatres were called upon to provide sound effects for what was appearing on the screen. As a result, a drummer's "trap" case held not only sticks, brushes, cymbals and stands, but an array of effects ranging from lion roars, cow moos, train whistles, and gun shots, to any imaginable effect a drummer could devise. The term "trap" (case, set, etc.) actually came from short-

days of sound pictures he developed such a technique of producing queer noise simulations that he was much in demand at the New York studios. He helped make one of the first sound recordings for a Walt Disney's animated cartoon *(Steamboat Willie?)* and did splendidly until he had to double for a parrot's voice. He swallowed the gadget used for this purpose and had some job getting it up on dry land again. His colleagues believe he let go of the thing when he suddenly thought of some brilliant idea for an invention". [11]

Billy continued to wow the audiences at the Capitol Theatre when S. L. "Roxy" Rothafel was brought in as Producer of Stage Shows in order to liven up a stale repertoire. Major Edwin C. Bowes was still the Managing Director, but "Roxy" was given full autonomy in the selection of the acts that

S.L. "Roxy" Rothafel,
Courtesy Radio City Music Hall

[10] "Stars of the Capitol" *Leedy Drum Topics*, no. 21, Leedy Manufacturing Company, Elkhart, IN, 1931

[11] "He Makes Money" by Alan Finn, *Mechanix Illustrated,* vol.12 no. 3, Fawcett Publications Inc., Louisville, KY, 1939

appeared at the Capitol. "Roxy" Rothafel's success at the Capitol Theatre encouraged him to open his own theatre, the Roxy on 7th Avenue in 1927. Rothafel had a special eye for talent. It was Rothafel that discovered the Radio City Music Hall Rockettes. "The Rockettes were born in 1925 when Russell Market of St. Louis, selected 16 dancing girls and formed the 'Sixteen Missouri Rockets'. This precision dancing team was so well received

Russel Market, Courtesy Radio City Music Hall

"Sixteen Missouri Rockets", Courtesy Radio City Music Hall

that they began to tour the country, ending up in New York City, where 'Roxy' Rothafel had a chance to see them. Deciding that he wanted them for his new Roxy Theatre, he doubled the size of the group, renaming them 'Russell E. Market's 32 Roxyettes'. When Roxy moved to the (Radio City) Music Hall, he expanded the dancing line to 36 girls to better fit the stage. They remained the 'Roxyettes' until 1935 when Roxy left Radio City and (Russell) Market decided upon a feminized version of the original name, forming their current name, the 'Rockettes'".

"In 1928, John D. Rockefeller, Jr. leased the land (between 47th and 52nd Streets, from Fifth Avenue to midway between the Avenue of the Americas and Seventh Street) from Columbia University, planning to turn it over to the Metropolitan Opera Company for a new opera house. Soon after the lease was signed came the Great Stock Market Crash. The plans for the new opera house were abandoned, and Mr. Rockefeller was left with an expensive piece of property. He soon decided to build a 'City Within a City', based on the theme of human optimism and progress, as a sign of hope in the midst of the Depression. One of the finest and largest tenants of the new complex was the Radio Corporation of America (RCA), and the center soon took the nickname 'Radio City'. Not long afterwards, the International Music Hall became known as Radio City Music Hall".

The Rockettes, Courtesy Radio City Music Hall.

Rockefeller assembled a team of the finest engineers, designers, artists, and decorators for the Music Hall. "When asked to design the auditorium for Radio City, Samuel 'Roxy' Rothafel, who, in his time (was) one of the greatest authorities on theatre design, travelled to Europe to study the designs of the great theatres overseas. He formed his inspiration, however, not in Europe but while on his return trip. He tells the story of watching the sun setting over the water from his ocean liner, and knowing that was the look he wanted to achieve in the Radio City auditorium. One good look at the auditorium shows that he was successful; the stage actually resembles a sun setting over a red velvet ocean of seats.

The Radio City Music Hall, appropriately called "The Showplace of the Nation," is a part of Rockefeller Center, the largest building project ever undertaken by private capital. Rockefeller Center is indeed a city within a city. Beneath the lofty, majestic pinnacles of its towers are beautiful roof gardens, spacious and luxurious theatres, broadcasting studios, exhibitions, offices, and a huge shopping center. The site occupies a full twelve acres in the heart of Manhattan, nearly all of the three city blocks from 48th to 51st Streets between Fifth and Sixth Avenues. Actual work on Rockefeller Center began on May 17, 1930. Since then, on a site formerly occupied by 229 small structures, ten buildings have been erected out of the total of fourteen planned for the gigantic development. The great buildings house a population of over 25,000 workers.

Rockefeller Center "A City Within a City", Courtesy Radio City Music Hall

DeWolfe Hopper, to name a few. The first show lasted over three hours, yet it did not include a motion picture, which was later added as a regular feature at the hall. The Music Hall is the only theatre to have accommodated more than 255,000,000 people in its history-more than the total US population"[12]. "Roxy" Rothafel was appointed as Director of the theatre with a managing staff of more than twenty-one people including Russell Market, founder of the then Roxyettes and Erno Rapee, Musical Director. Rothafel brought both Market and Rapee to Radio City from his Roxy Theatre. Rapee, in turn, assembled a staff of seventy-five of the finest musicians available in New York including of course, his prodigy, Billy Gladstone.

On December 27, 1932, Radio City Music Hall opened its doors to the world for the very first time, welcoming an audience of almost 6,000 people including many prominent leaders of the nation's political, financial, social and theatrical life-to its premiere. Opening night featured a dazzling lineup that included stars such as Weber & Fields, Jan Peerce, Martha Graham, Ray Bolger, Gertrude Nielsen, The Tuskegee Institute Choir, and

Radio City Music Hall Auditorium, Courtesy Radio City Music Hall

[12] *Showplace of the Nation*, Radio City Music Hall Productions, New York, NY, 1989

The first year's attendance at the Music Hall was a world record-breaking six million. Weary Depression-laden audiences needed a break from

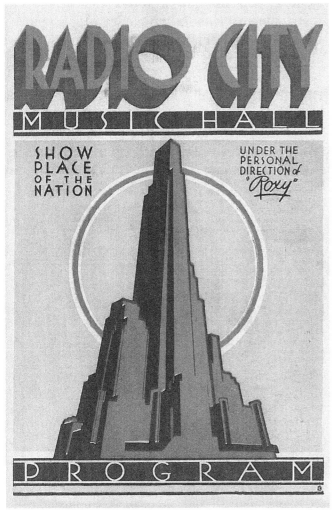

Radio City Music Hall first year program, notice "Under the Personal Direction of 'Roxy'", Courtesy Radio City Music Hall

their woes and the Music Hall was just the ticket. As a result, the dapper, handsome Gladstone with a pen-

chant for spirited, eye-catching high-sticking, caught the attention of burgeoning audiences. Buddy Rich recalls, "He had his drums very high...because he was a showman, and he would raise his hands (but) his concept was totally legitimate. I used to sit in the last seat in the last row of the balcony at Radio City Music Hall and listen to him articulate off the snare drum. Every stroke was like an arrow...without the slightest bit of motion he could almost shatter your eardrum. He had that kind of technique. When he played a roll, you couldn't tell if it was a roll or if he only had one stick on the drum. It was that pure". We drummers strive to obtain an even sound from both sticks on a drum, pitch-matching sticks, striking the drum at equal areas of the head, comparable stick height, etc. Using the "matched" grip will naturally result in a more even sound. The "traditional" grip requires more effort to achieve an even sound simply because of the different physical contact the opposing grips apply to the sticks. Rich's point is that Gladstone's roll was so pure, it did not sound as though he was alternating strokes between his hands. Ed Shaughnessy continues, "I was an avid fan of (Gladstone) when I was a teenager and looked forward to hearing him play at Radio City Music Hall with great enthusiasm. His masterful, flowing playing, combined with great showmanship, was a treat for the eye and the ear. Billy was an early exponent of the graceful, smooth and flowing style of drumming that I also heard and saw later in Jo Jones, Sid Catlett, Buddy Rich and Dave Tough on the full drum set. He drew the sound from the drum and used a relaxed and open grip which resulted in the beautiful, full sound for which he was famous. Billy was a class man with a class style who left a legacy that enriched us all".[13]

The Music Hall Staff, Courtesy Radio City Music Hall

---

[13] "Billy Remembered" *Modern Drummer,* vol. 5 no. 7 Modern Drummer Publications, Inc., Ceder Grove, NJ, 1981

Gladstone continued as a Leedy endorser and is shown in a January 1933 Leedy Manufacturing Company advertisement. "Bill Gladstone has been selected as the first drummer of this great theatre orchestra (Radio City Music Hall)- a distinction richly deserved for Bill is one of America's really great drum players. He says that Leedy instruments have been an important factor in his success. Radio City, too has chosen Leedy equipment, including kettle drums, xylophones and bells for both of its theatres".[14] Albeit a bit self-congratulatory, the copy does note a richly deserved distinction for one of America's really great drum players.

Gladstone Leedy Endorsement,
Courtesy Rob Cook

Arthur Press, educator, retired percussionist for the Boston Symphony Orchestra, and former Gladstone student who eventually followed Billy in the Radio City Music Hall Orchestra, also vividly recalls his first impression of Gladstone. "I was taken to the Radio City Music Hall in the early 40's when I was 13 years old. That of course was an incredible time for the Music Hall. It was newly built and was 'The Showplace of the Nation' as they called themselves. To see the stage come up from nowhere (on hydraulic lifts, more later) and see this tall, handsome guy standing at dress attention for probably the whole show, was really something. Billy was married to a Rockette (former Dorothy Frank). Their apartment had no kitchen. I mean, there was a kitchen with a stove, but for all intents and purposes, Billy and his wife ate out most of the time. Their whole life was the Music Hall. (As a performer) you got to the Music Hall by 12:30PM and basically spent all your time there. There was a two-hour break between shows. The (movie) feature started at 10:30AM and the first show was somewhere around 12:30. Then every two hours after that there was

another show (to play). You started your day at 12:30 and ended at 10:30. Since there wasn't too much you could do (at mealtime) you ended up spending your time in the Music Hall cafeteria or going out to eat with the guys and the girls and having a quick early dinner after the second show. That was (Billy's) whole life. The kitchen is where he had his gut snares hanging. He'd soak them and then hang them out to dry using the flat irons from a Chinese laundry as weights (to keep the drying gut from curling). After which, he would shellac them so they would have the right kind of brittle quality, producing the best sound". Billy's kitchen was famous among his close fraternity of drum associ-

Radio City Music Hall Cafeteria, Courtesy Radio City Music Hall

ates. Eddie Jenkins, drummer for the Bunny Berigan Orchestra and former Gladstone student recalls, "Too bad you can't show the inside of the refrigerator. It was like a miniature hardware store. I had only one brief peek into it (and) the contents were not the usual milk, bread, cold cuts, etc., but rather little containers of nuts, bolts, washers and other hardware items not usually found in a household refrigerator. I don't even remember whether it was hooked up to the electrical outlet (i.e., cold inside)".

With the demanding schedule of the Music Hall, Billy's patent applications took a brief respite, though his inventive mind flourished. It was the Music Hall and Gladstone's ensuing global success that inspired him further. "'I am now bringing to fruition a lot of ideas that have been tucked away too long in my head'. Billy says he didn't start to click with his inventions until he went to the Music Hall in 1932. 'Maybe it was because I never

---

[14] "The Choice of Radio City" , Leedy Manufacturing Company Advertisement, 1933

got discouraged. Maybe I was due for a break. I dare say I wasn't ready before 1932 to cash in. I don't know. As soon as those sticks begin to fly from the percussions something magic touches off a spark in my head. It's Aladdin-lamp like. Ideas start to pop. I get all steamed up'. Sometimes too, Billy gets so steamed up that he forgets to turn the pages of his music as he sits in the great Music Hall orchestra pit. Or slips momentarily into 'inventor's sleep', but Maestro Rapee just smiles understandingly. Billy follows Mr. Rapee's baton with slightly more than a musician's eye. He follows it with a proud and loving eye. He is the inventor of the Rapee baton. The patent is pending (though never granted), but the baton has been manufactured for a year and a half anyway, bringing him hundreds of dollars in royalties. The Music

Gladstone holding Rapee Baton in right hand, Tongue Depressor in left,
Courtesy *Home Mechanix*, Times Mirror, formerly *Mechanix Illustrated*, Fawcett Publications

Hall audience sees little of the baton. It's part of the idea. The baton glows in the dark, its tip visible from all parts of the theatre but its full length (of light) exposed only to the musicians and stage performers. This effect is obtained by the use of Lucite, a transparent material which is illuminated by reflection internally. The light is provided by a small flashlight battery in the handle of the baton. Billy says the idea came to him when he saw that an ordinary baton was not always visible at once to the entire orchestra. He also knew that Maestro Rapee was rough on wooden sticks, breaking one or two daily. His (pending, but not granted) patented baton, however, is virtually unbreakable. Besides Mr. Rapee, Rudy Vallee, Edwin Franko Goldman and other conductors have adopted it. By extending the handle end of the luminous baton, Billy turned it into a new kind of blackboard pointer which is being

used in schools and lecture halls. More royalties! Using the same principal of reflection, he also invented a tongue depressor, which is a veritable boon to throat doctors. This small device not only presses down the tongue but provides the light at the same time. The material is Pirex [sic] rather than Lucite for sterilizing purposes. This (pending, but not granted) patented depressor is used in the Music Hall and by several New York specialists. A surgical instrument company has begun to manufacture it on a large scale".[15]

One can only imagine the Music Hall itself was an inspiration to Gladstone's inventive genius. Consider, "The Great Stage was designed with the intention of creating the most elaborate and best equipped stage in the world. It measures a staggering 144 feet across and $66^{1/2}$ feet deep-yet more spectacular than its immense size is the wide variety of special effects that can be created upon it. What makes the stage so versatile, so technically superior to other stages, is its ingenious design. It is comprised of 3 elevators which can be operated separately or as a single unit. Each is 70 feet wide and can be raised 13 feet above, and lowered 27 feet below stage level. There is also a 'pit' elevator which juts out in front of the stage and responsible for transporting the orchestra (cue Billy!) from the basement to the stage level. In addition, in the center of the stage is an actual 43' diameter turntable, which is used for special effects and quick scene changes. Over the years the stage has supported everything from a puffing locomotive, to processions of elephants, camels, sheep, and donkeys, to a 14,000 gallon swimming pool. This may seem incredible but each elevator is capable of lifting 27 tons! As ingenious as the design of the stage itself, is the hydraulic system that operates it. A 300 horsepower motor, a centrifugal force pump and a 28,000 gallon tank of hydraulic fluid compressed to 250 pounds per square inch comprise this sophisticated system and allow the elevators to raise and lower. This hydraulic sys-

The Great Stage Control Board
Courtesy Radio City Music Hall

---

15 "He Makes Money" by Alan Finn, *Mechanix Illustrated*, vol.12 no. 3 Fawcett Publications Inc., Louisville, KY, 1939

The Great Stage Light Console, Courtesy Radio City Music Hall

Spanish felt. To aid the player in quickly selecting the correct pair from his pile of mallets, Gladstone added different colored tips that corresponded to the various types and densities of beater heads. When Gretsch Manufacturing Company included Gladstone mallets in their 1939 drum catalogue, they noted the endorsement of "Such world-famous percussion artists as: San Herman, 'Red' Norvo, Yoichi Hiraoka, Milton Schlessinger, Dillon Ober, Dave Grupp, Joe Castka, Karl Glassman, Ray Gomar, Dave Gusikoff and dozens of other brilliant performers (who) use and enthusiastically endorse GRETSCH-GLADSTONE Percussion Mallets. Their fine tone-production and matchless playing qualities are a positive help to better technique. Invented by a great artist for the benefit of every brother artist-give them a try"![18]

tem eventually became the model for the elevators used on Navy air-craft carriers during World War II. The system was so 'classified' that during the war, the United States Government felt it necessary to keep a watch over the basement of Radio City in case an enemy agent should sneak down during intermission for a 'peek'"[16]

Also keeping watch over all these engineering marvels was Billy's inventive eye. Thus, his patent sabbatical ended less than two years later when he was granted a patent (number 2,040,603) for a "Hammer for Percussion Musical Instruments" commonly referred to as xylophone mallets. In the treatise of the patent "The handles of the percussion now employed are made of rattan, but those possess many disadvantages among which may be mentioned their non-uniformity and non-rapidity of resiliency, their property of remaining bent instead of returning to a straight position, their loss of resiliency and flexibility during use and their brittleness resulting in their being frequently broken during use".[17] To combat these negative effects, though not limiting himself to any particular material in the patent, Gladstone designed hollow handled shafts made of celluloid with beater heads made with Pyralin, rubber, and Latex impregnated

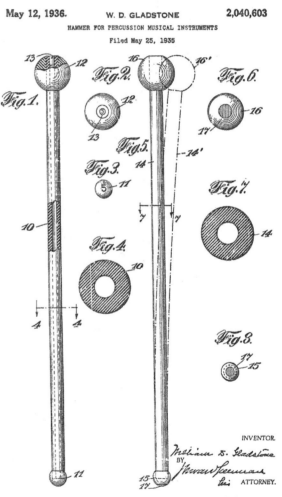

"Hammer for Percussion Musical Instruments" patent drawing,
Author's collection

[16] *Showplace of the Nation*, Radio City Music Hall Productions, New York, NY, 1989

[17] "Hammer For Percussion Musical Instruments" United States Patent Office, no. 2,040,603,Washington, DC, 1936

[18] The Fred Gretsch Manufacturing Company catalogue, Brooklyn, NY, 1939

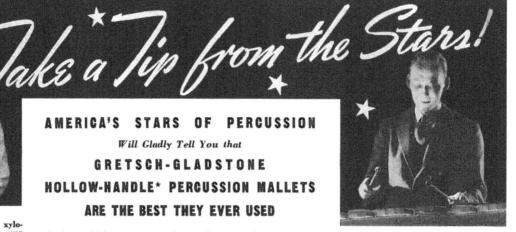

Take a Tip from the Stars!

SAM HERMAN
The world's greatest xylophonist and a favorite over the air.

WILLIAM D. GLADSTONE
Star drummer of Erno Rapee's Radio City Music Hall Symphony Orchestra, inventor of the patented hollow handle percussion mallet.

AMERICA'S STARS OF PERCUSSION

Will Gladly Tell You that

GRETSCH-GLADSTONE
HOLLOW-HANDLE* PERCUSSION MALLETS
ARE THE BEST THEY EVER USED

Such world-famous percussion artists as: Sam Herman, "Red" Norvo, Yoichi Hiraoka, Milton Schlessinger, Dillon Ober, Dave Grupp, Joe Castka, Karl Glassman, Ray Gomar, Dave Gusikoff and dozens of other brilliant performers use and enthusiastically endorse GRETSCH-GLADSTONE Percussion Mallets. Their fine tone-production and matchless playing qualities are a positive help to better technique. Invented by a great artist for the benefit of every brother artist—give them a trial!

* U. S. Patent No. 2040603

YOICHI HIRAOKA
Master of the Xylophone and broadcasting artist.

"RED" NORVO
The greatest swing-man of them all, with technique all his own.

Gretsch-Gladstone Hollow Handle Percussion Mallets, Author's collection

'BILLY' GLADSTONE
—master drummer and inventive genius, with Erno Rapee's Radio City Music Hall Symphony Orchestra, inventor of the Hollow Handle Percussion Mallets

GRETSCH-GLADSTONE
HOLLOW-HANDLE PERCUSSION MALLETS
U. S. PATENT NO. 2040603

ARE "TOPS" WITH AMERICA'S TOP-RANKERS

Such world-famous percussion artists as: Sam Herman, "Red" Norvo, Yoichi Hiraoka, Milton Schlessinger, Dillon Ober, Dave Grupp, Joe Castka, Karl Glassman, Ray Gomar, Chauncey Morehouse, Dave Gusikoff and dozens of other brilliant performers use and enthusiastically endorse GRETSCH-GLADSTONE Mallets.

UNIFORM RESILIENCE • PERFECT BALANCE • LONGER LIFE!

Supremely *right* in every respect, the patented HOLLOW-HANDLE Mallet appeals instantly to every percussion player. Here's exactly the *right* resilience for brilliant technique, just the *right* resistance, precisely the *right* 'give'. This perfect resilience is absolutely uniform and unchanging in *all* GRETSCH-GLADSTONE mallets. They last longer than the best rattan. They balance more truly. And their beauty is permanent. For the sake of your own professional success.

Ask Your Music Dealer or Write for Descriptive Price List

THE FRED. GRETSCH MFG. CO.

Musical Instrument Makers Since 1883

529 So. Wabash Av., CHICAGO, ILL. • 60 Broadway, BROOKLYN, N. Y.

October 1937 The Metronome, Author's collection

Gretsch-Gladstone mallets, Author's collection

Billy's next patent ("Key Carrier", number 2,066,526), granted in 1937, was a direct result from an encounter at the Music Hall. "For 10 years Billy tried to work out a nebulous scheme for a key holder that would not bulge in the pocket and yet would be at once handy and simple to manufacture

Gladstone Keycase, Courtesy *Home Mechanix*, Times Mirror, formerly *Mechanix Illustrated*, Fawcett Publications

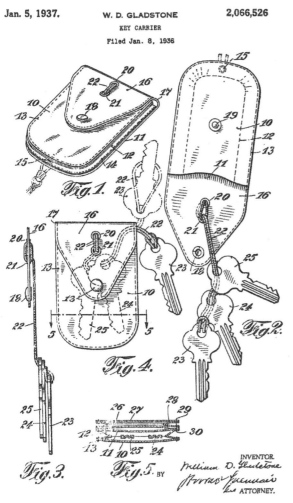

Jan. 5, 1937.   W. D. GLADSTONE   2,066,526
KEY CARRIER
Filed Jan. 8, 1936

Fig.1. *Fig.2.* *Fig.3.* *Fig.4.* *Fig.5.*

INVENTOR.
William D. Gladstone
BY
ATTORNEY.

"Key Carrier" patent drawing, Author's collection

...one day a woman harpist at the Music Hall dropped her change purse, spilling out in the pit several keys in addition to some coins. Billy picked up the keys and strung them on a small chain which he attached to an empty key case he carried. 'This'll do until I get my own key case invented', he told her. By a curious quirk of fate, he had accidentally struck upon the thing he had been wracking his head for. The makeshift key case attracted attention in the orchestra. Other musicians, thinking he had realized his invention, asked him for cases. Billy borrowed the harpist's key case, put some coins in with the keys, and took it around to a model maker. The model proved satisfactory and the Gladstone key case hit the market with an immediate favorable response. The device is now being pushed all over the world (including Wanamakers, his first US job) and fat checks are coming in regularly. The chances are that Billy Gladstone could sit back and live on his accumulated royalties and his inventive genius,

for the income from his musical creations alone run into a substantial figure. But drums are his first love and he can't leave them alone".[19] It should be noted that the Gladstone Key Case is still available today.

Gladstone Keycase, Author's collection

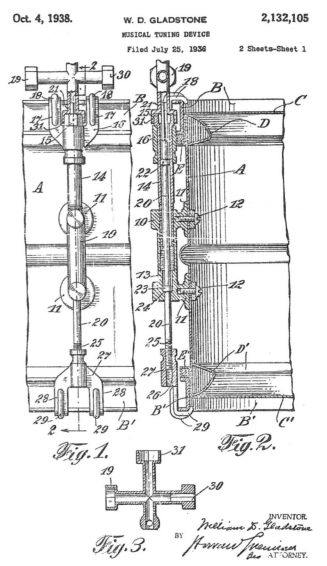

Oct. 4, 1938.   W. D. GLADSTONE   2,132,105
MUSICAL TUNING DEVICE
Filed July 25, 1936   2 Sheets—Sheet 1

Fig.1. *Fig.2.* *Fig.3.*

INVENTOR.
William D. Gladstone
BY
ATTORNEY.

"Musical Tuning Device" patent drawing, Author's collection

Later that year Gladstone's endorsement deal took an abrupt turn. Maybe Leedy was too slow to react, or maybe because the Fred Gretsch Manufacturing Company offered a partnership, Billy's next patent ("Musical Tuning Device", number 2,132,105, later revised with number 2,172,578) was featured in a full-page advertisement on page three of the

[19] "He Makes Money" by Alan Finn, *Mechanix Illustrated,* vol.12 no. 3 Fawcett Publications, Inc., Louisville, KY, 1939

Premiere of the GRETSCH GLADSTONE Drum, Author's collection

exclusive franchises. To win such instantaneous and universal recognition, it is evident that this new drum must be revolutionary in design and performance. And so it is! Embodying utterly new and original construction-principals, all of them the personal invention of that master-drummer, William D. Gladstone-developed, tested and perfected under actual playing conditions in one of the most important and most exacting drum jobs in the whole United States, the GRETSCH-GLADSTONE DRUM brings to the artist-drummer tonal and technical advantages that no other drum in the world can offer. For the sake of your own personal career you should-you MUST-see and play this new drum. You'll find it a revelation"! Talk about compelling copy writing..."For the sake of your own professional career"(?). Dressed in a tuxedo, Billy has a dogged look of a proud father as he cradles his latest creation. Below, a caption reads: "William D. Gladstone master drummer

September 1937 edition of *The Metronome* magazine. Entitled "Now Try This One"! it reads "To those Artist-Drummers everywhere whose high professional attainments entitle them to the finest of instrumental equipment, regardless of price, Fred. Gretsch Manufacturing Company and Billy Gladstone present the GRETSCH-GLADSTONE DRUM the outstanding sensation of this year's Music Trades' Convention. Top-notch New York drummers flocked to see it-played it-*bought* it! Famous conductors heard it demonstrated and voiced unqualified praise. Music dealers from forty cities placed their orders and put in their requests for

and inventive genius with fifteen patents to his credit, is a featured favorite in Erno Rapee's Radio City Hall Symphonic Orchestra, where he has played drums ever since the opening of that famous house. Of his host of admirers the warmest perhaps are his fellow drummers, who give unstinted praise to Billy's professional career".[20] Oddly, all this flamboyant copy failed to explain the "revolutionary design". That came later on page 83 of this same edition of *The Metronome* in a feature article "Gladstone Invents Gadgets While Drumming". "At the New York Music Trades Convention, Billy was asked to appear for an hour...He stayed at the con-

[20] "Now Try This One"! Fred Gretsch Manufacturing Company advertisement, *The Metronome*, vol. 53, no. 9 Metronome Publishing Co., New York, NY, 1937

Gladstone Invents Gadgets While Drumming

MOST people watch the drummer in a band. And Billy Gladstone, the dapper drummer of the Music Hall Symphony Orchestra, takes some watching. While he's beating out a rousing finale for *Light Cavalry* overture, he's probably inventing a new kind of orange squeezer; and when he's tapping his tympani, he might be thinking of the patent rights on his new, simplified key case.

At the New York Musical Trades Convention, Billy was asked to appear for half an hour to display his new glass drum—a little thing he just thought up. He stayed at the convention four days, and displayed fourteen of his latest thirty-eight inventions.

Most of Billy's inventions are in the musical line.

For instance:

The new Billy Gladstone Snare Drum. This has seven improvements. The reason he invented it, Billy says, is because the old drum was not adequate for the new medium of radio and the new sound systems which have been installed in most places of entertainment. Some of the features include Billy's invention for tuning the drum as one would a violin. Heretofore, drummers tapped on the top drumhead of the drum to hear the tone, turned the drum over to tighten or loosen the tuning key, then turned it back rightside up again to tap and listen. This could go on for hours, Billy says. Now, the tuning key is adjusted on the drum's top, the snares are re-spaced so that they form a bridge like a violin's. He's equipped the drum with a number of stops or levers, similar to an organ's stops, whereby he can produce different tones—tom toms, rat-a-tats, boom booms, etc.—and this can be done while the drummer continues to play. He has a system of levers and buttons around the drumhead, and these are tapped with the drummer's stick as he continues to play in a changed tone or effect. A "remote control" button eliminates overtones picked up by a radio microphone while broadcasting.

Edwin Franko Goldman saw the drum exhibited at the convention, immediately ordered one in pearl and gold; the New York Philharmonic drummer bought one in satin chromium, Toscanini's drummer took one in chromium and brass, and Billy's own drum is of 24 carat gold.

The baton he invented looks like a glass stick. It lights up at the end, throwing off a miniature headlight. In a darkened auditorium the musicians in the pit and singers on the stage can follow the light as the conductor beats the tempo, but the audience does not see the light. It is unbreakable. Erno Rapee, Music Hall maestro, who is tough on batons and usually breaks two or more a day, uses one now. It is made of a new duPont material called lucite.

Glass Drum

This same material was used by Gladstone to make what looks like a glass drum. This has artistic and entertainment value, by virtue of the lighting effects which may be used inside the transparent drum.

He has invented three sets of mallets for the xylophone, marimbaphone and vibraharp, making them out of fiberloids, the material used by golf club manufacturers to cover the steel shafts of the clubs. By making the mallets hollow, Billy gets tone, flexibility and balance. The three sets are of different weights, so Billy put different colored buttons on the mallets, so that a player can grab the ones he wants quickly.

The Metronome, September, 1937

And just to fill in some spare time, he invented a transparent trap drummer's table—which covers a drummer's whole outfit but does not conceal it from an audience. Audiences are very curious about drummers and their gadgets. They like to see everything, fascinated by the drummer's equipment and performance.

His Flexible High Hat Cymbals are hooked onto the drum, attached to a flexible cable, and are worked with a foot pedal. He invented the Swish Brush, used by jam bands and swing outfits. This is a little cylinder with a button on each end. Push the red button, a long wire brush comes out of one end. Push the green button, a shorter wire brush comes out of the other end. The brushes are used to swish against the drums and cymbals.

Operating on the principle involved in the automobile self-starter, he invented the Automatic Vibraphone Switch. As soon as the pedal is pushed, the vibraphone motor starts automatically.

The Scotch Sticks are for special use in bagpipe bands and in playing martial music. They have hollow handles and will last a lifetime, which, says Billy, is another reason for their name.

He has invented a new kind of mallet to play on the drummer's bells. They are transparent, hollow and create a celeste effect. The "Flash Cymbals," he devised are plated in chromium, placed on aluminum sticks, and are flashy in a jam band when hit by a spotlight.

His key case, a favorite at Black, Starr and Frost-Gorham and Parker and Battersby's, is on a chain which attaches itself to the belt loop of a man's trousers and stretches to the trouser's pocket. He evolved a simple way of stringing the keys ordinarily carried and one key locks all the rest in the case.

He is now working on a gadget to turn the pages of the drummer's music on the music stand. Often, he says he gets to thinking of an invention while he is playing and forgets to turn the pages. So, any minute now, the Page Turner.

INVENTOR — MUSICIAN

Billy Gladstone (drummer at Radio City Music Hall) and Fred Gretsch III inspect the new Gladstone Drums at the New York Trade Convention.

Defonso Piano Accordionola

A new musical instrument that combines features of the piano and accordion. One of the models is produced in four varying shifts of tone; one, two, three, or six. The stops are selected to interpret a variety of timbres; the true accordion, violin, saxophone, oboe, piccolo, and organ, etc.

The Piano Accordionola is adaptable to homes, radio, concert, church and orchestra. The console cabinet is finished in grained hard wood, and for use in orchestras, this instrument can also be made portable. For further information write to: National Accordion Mfg. Co., 206 Stanwix St., Pittsburgh, Pa.

Recording Service

Harry Smith, former chief recording engineer for Brunswick, Columbia and American Recording Corporation, is now conducting a studio devoted to individual recordings. Studio, located at 156 West 44th Street, New York City, has installed a regular phonograph recording equipment. Equipped to take programs off the air, and to record dates at the studio. The "off the air" service is especially helpful to bands playing out of town but whose programs come over networks heard in New York. Bands availing themselves of Harry Smith's recording service are:—Bob Crosby, Russ Morgan, Glen Miller, Shep Fields, Tommy Dorsey and many others.

September 1937 The Metronome, Author's collection

Goldman Goes GRETSCH GLADSTONE, Author's collection

vention, immediately ordered one in pearl and gold; the New York Philharmonic drummer bought one in satin chromium, Toscanini's drummer took one in chromium and brass, and Billy's own drum is of 24 carat gold".[21] Several other reasons have been cited for the inspiration of the three-way tuning mechanism. "Bob Stuart, retired percussionist from the United States Marine Band recalls, 'I was one of the substitute percussionists at Radio City, where the pit was so small you barely had room to move. Billy told me he designed his tensioning system simply because there wasn't room on stage to turn the drum over'. All drum heads in those days were made of calfskin and, depending on climatic conditions, required constant tensioning. Gladstone's

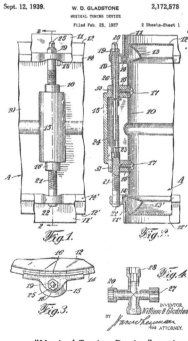

Roller skate mechanism that inspired Gladstone's patent, Author's collection, photo by Nick Falzerano

unique three-way tensioning, whereby both heads could be tensioned from the top lug (consequently) the drum would not have to be removed from the stand in order to tension the bottom head".[22] One can only imagine the effects of moving a calf-head drum from the basement of the Music Hall to stage

Sept. 12, 1939.   W. D. GLADSTONE   2,172,578
MUSICAL TUNING DEVICE
Filed Feb. 25, 1937   2 Sheets-Sheet 1

Fig.1.   Fig.2.   Fig.3.   Fig.4.

INVENTOR
William D. Gladstone
BY James Keyman
ATTORNEY

"Musical Tuning Device" revised patent drawing, Author's collection

---

vention four days, and displayed fourteen of his latest thirty-eight inventions. The new Billy Gladstone Snare Drum...has seven improvements. The reason he invented it, Billy says, is because the old drum was not adequate for the new medium of radio and the new sound systems which have been installed in most places of entertainment. Some of the features include Billy's invention for tuning the drum as one would a violin. Heretofore, drummers tapped on the top drumhead of the drum to hear the tone, turned the drum over to tighten or loosen (the bottom head) then turn it back rightside up again to tap again and listen. This could go on for hours, Billy says. Edwin Franko Goldman saw the drum exhibited at the con-

21 "Gladstone Invents Gadgets While Drumming" *The Metronome*, vol. 53, no. 9 Metronome Publishing Co., New York, NY, 1937
22 "Billy Gladstone Custom Drums" by Chet Falzerano, Percussive Notes, vol. 32, no. 4, Percussive Arts Society, Lawton, OK, 1994

THE ARISTOCRAT OF DRUMS

IS THE BRILLIANT NEW

GRETSCH-GLADSTONE ORCHESTRA DRUM

BRINGING YOU **3** GENUINELY NEW FEATURES FOR PLUS - PERFORMANCE

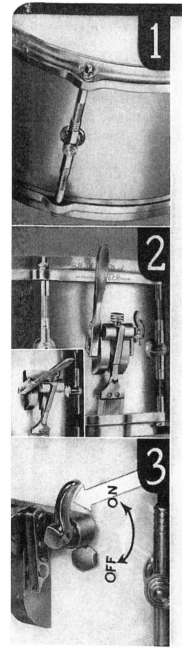

1 — 3-WAY TENSIONING

For convenience, accuracy and speed of tuning, the unique GRETSCH-GLADSTONE tensioning-principle stands alone! It gives you —

I. Separate tensioning of batter head,
II. Separate tensioning of snare head, and
III. Simultaneous tensioning of both heads at once

— and all three adjustments made from the top (batter side) without removing the drum from the stand!

■

2 — PERFECTED SNARE-CONTROL

Lightning-fast and smooth as silk in action, here at last is a throw-off that actually operates by a mere tap of the drumstick. What's equally important is that it's done in a natural easy motion without changing your grip of the stick in the slightest. And the entire make-up of this strainer is so simple and so rugged that dependable operation is a certainty. The better the drummer the more he'll appreciate this contribution to finer drum-technique.

■

3 — FINGERTIP TONE-REGULATION

Just a touch of the finger lever, conveniently located in the snare-strainer base, eliminates or restores at will the overtones (or "ring") found in every drum. Whatever tone-quality you want it's yours — INSTANTLY! Extreme delicacy and crispness of tone for recording and broadcasting — full power, tremendous power when you want to "pour it in" — and a host of novel and interesting effects as well, yours to command!

WILLIAM D. GLADSTONE (his thousands of friends and admirers call him, "BILLY") is a featured favorite with Erno Rappee's Radio City Music Hall Symphony Orchestra where he has played drums ever since the opening of that famous New York house. Enjoying world-wide reputation of his own as one of the outstanding drum artists of our times, Mr. Gladstone is an inventive genius as well, with 15 patents already to his credit.

■

A TRIUMPH OF TEAMWORK

Conceived in the active mind of one of America's top-ranking drum artists and brought to reality in America's oldest existing drum factory, the new GRETSCH-GLADSTONE DRUM is truly a triumph of teamwork!

The tremendous, practical utility of the WILLIAM D. GLADSTONE improvements (developed, perfected and proven under actual playing conditions in one of the most exacting drum jobs in the whole United States) put this new drum above and beyond comparison.

Freed by this *precision* instrument from the troublesome uncertainties of temperature and humidity, the artist-drummer will rejoice in the brilliant, sensitive response of his GRETSCH-GLADSTONE DRUM. He will delight in the speed and accuracy of its unique adjustments. And that glorious feeling of complete control of his instrument that comes to the player of a GRETSCH-GLADSTONE DRUM is inevitably reflected in improved technique and showmanship.

This is, frankly, a drum for seasoned artists—for men of preeminent standing in their profession who feel themselves limited in their progress by the handicaps of commonplace equipment.

To such men we say: Here's the drum you've always wanted. It's the answer to your problem. And we are just waiting for you to write us— "Where can I see it?" We'll do the rest—and without the slightest obligation to you!

FRED. GRETSCH
MANUFACTURING COMPANY

Musical Instrument Makers, Since 1883

60 BROADWAY, BROOKLYN, N. Y.
529 SO. WABASH AVENUE, CHICAGO, ILLINOIS

The Aristocrat of Drums, January 1938 *The Metronome,* Author's collection

Three Aces, February 1938 *The Metronome,* Author's collection

level via the orchestra pit elevator. The change in temperature and humidity would substantially change the settings of the calf skin heads. Gladstone's design allowed him to make rapid changes to both heads from the top of the drum.

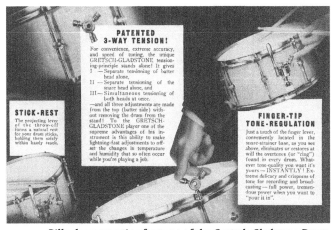

Billy demonstrating features of the Gretsch-Gladstone Drum,
Author's collection

Gladstone got the tension idea from the clamping mechanism of old roller skates. He elaborated on the idea by permitting the tightening of each head individually, as well as both in unison. The large top tension rod with a hex head screwed into the lug, thereby tensioning the top head. Through its hollow center passed a smaller tension rod with a standard square head on the top. Inside the lug this rod engaged the bottom tension rod. The bottom tension rod screwed into the lug with a left-hand thread, thereby facilitating a clockwise tightening from the top. Since both tension rods move toward, or away from each other, during this tensioning process, a differential mechanism was required. Gladstone's patent shows the top inner rod ending in a hex shaft. The bottom tension rod had a corresponding hex socket, allowing the two shafts to engage throughout the tightening/loosening process. When the Gretsch-Gladstone snare drum went into production, a more simplified tongue-and-groove mechanism was utilized. Rather than the top rod ending with a hex shaft, the Gretsch design incorporated a flat blade. The bottom tension rod had a corresponding engaging slot. Though not as sophisticated as the original patent design, the Gretsch-Gladstone sliding differential accomplished its intended purpose. Continued use though, often resulted in this differential hanging-up, or breaking. Gladstone also designed a special three-way key to fit the top tension rod nuts. Attached to the side of the drum on a hollow post that also served as an air vent, this key had three sockets. A hex-shaped socket to fit the outer part of the top tension rod, a square-shaped one to fit the inner bottom rod, and a socket combining both. This socket facilitated tensioning of both heads in unison.

Each of the sockets were incised with laeral grooves, one groove on the top socket, two on the bottom socket and three on the combination socket. This aided the player to identify the correct socket even in the dark. The Gretsch-Gladstone snare drum included several other

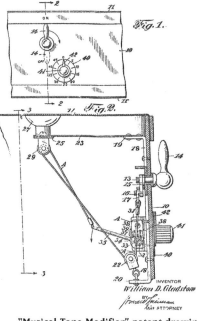

"Musical Tone Modifier" patent drawing,
Author's collection

features. The advantage of his throw-off ("Perfected Snare Control") was that it could be activated with a tap of the drumstick without changing the player's grip. The throw-off lever extended above the top rim enabling the

Gretsch-Gladstone gut butt plate, Author's collection

player to engage or disengage the snares by striking the lever with the drum stick. Billy's students report seeing him flip snares on and off with unbelievably rapid speed, as he performed equally unbelievable licks. Incorporated in the base of the throw off is the patented Gladstone internal tone control ("Finger Tip Tone Regulation"). Several years after the Gretsch-Gladstone snare drum was introduced, Gladstone was granted a patent ("Musical Tone Modifier", number 2,495,450, revised with number 2,495,451) for a design that dampened the unwanted ring of the snare drum. The pads that pressed against the drum head to muffle the drum were rubber suction cups rather than the common felt used by other manufacturers. His design also enabled the player to flip these pads on and off rapidly. Other manufacturers engaged the tone control with a threaded

POSITIVE THROW-OFF

This up-side-down photograph shows the complete and positive action of the GRETSCH-GLADSTONE throw-off. As you can see, there's no chance of accidental snare-response when you've released the snares.

"No chance of accidental snare response", Author's collection

knob that pulled the pads up to the head. This required several turns and was therefore much slower to engage. Gladstone's spring-loaded pads were virtually instantaneous. The butt plate on the gut snare-equipped drum was unusual as well. Billy preferred gut snares. To achieve equal tension for each strand of gut, the butt was designed so each pair of gut was pulled through the plate, then held in place by tensioning a set screw against them. Drums equipped with wire snares had a standard pinch plate butt. However, the straps holding the wire snares had a thin spring steel insert inside so the snares would always be forced away from the drum when thrown off, even when the drum was upside down. The Gretsch-Gladstone snare drum was offered in a second configuration, with two-way tensioning and minus the Gladstone fingertip tone control. Oddly, though it was tensioned like any other drum, either from the top or the bottom, the tension rods were formed with the characteristic two-stepped top. The rod, however, was one solid unit. Since it did not require the special three-way key, this top was apparently only a decoration. The 1939 Gretsch catalogue said that this model was offered to those whose "budget doesn't run just now to the 'full feature' model". Duke Kramer, who joined the Gretsch organization in 1935, qualifies further "Some drummers didn't want the three-way tuning. They didn't mind turning the drum over to tune the bottom head".

Gretsch-Gladstone 2-Way Drum, Author's collection

GRETSCH-GLADSTONE SINGLE TENSION BASS DRUMS
With the Gladstone "Finger-Tip" Tone Regulation

JOSEPH CASTKA
Bass Drummer with Erno Rapee's
Radio City Music Hall Orchestra

AUGUST ("GUS") HELMECKE
Bass Drummer of Goldman's Band,
formerly with John Phillip Sousa

Like all GRETSCH-GLADSTONE equipment this superb drum brings the artist genuine and practical advantages that make it an essential in every top-ranking drummer's outfit. Starting out with sturdy construction, handsome finish and workmanship, and perfect mechanical action, this drum adds a completeness and rapidity of Tone Control positively not to be found on any other bass drum. Two conveniently located levers, operated by a mere "Finger Tip" touch, apply or release the Gretsch tone controls. Each head has its own individual control and either or both can be instantly applied or released, giving you the choice of full-tone, semi-tone or completely muted tone in a second!

PRICES AND FINISHES

Though regularly built and stocked only in the four standard sizes listed here, we will gladly quote prices for special sizes on request. Shells come in your choice of dark mahogany or the many beautiful "Dress Parade" finishes described on Pages 10 and 11. Metal parts are polished chromium plated.

Shell	Duco Fin.	Gretsch-Pearl
26"x12"	5M8040—$100.00D	5M8045—$120.00D
26"x14"	5M8041— 102.50D	5M8046— 122.50D
28"x12"	5M8042— 105.00D	5M8047— 125.00D
28"x14"	5M8043— 107.50D	5M8048— 127.50D

Featuring — Gretsch-Gladstone "Finger Tip" Tone Regulation applying to each head and semi-automatic in action . . . 3-ply laminated shells . . . Finest tone-matched calf heads, pure white and hard-finished . . . choice of beautiful "Dress Parade" finishes . . . Gretsch-Pearl Inlaid Hoops . . . true bass drum tone, 100% controlled . . . . .

Gretsch-Gladstone Bass Drum, Author's collection

GRETSCH-GLADSTONE TUNABLE TOM TOMS
Featuring the Gladstone "Finger-Tip" Tone Regulation

Every GRETSCH-GLADSTONE owner will want a set of these distinguished new tom toms. Not because in their flashing beauty these tom toms match the rest of their equipment, not just because they are sturdy in build and superfine in tone, but above all because they give original, brilliant tonal effects not obtainable with any other tom toms of any kind. With fast, semi-automatic action to tune for all playing conditions, these tom toms offer in addition the fabulous "Finger Tip" Tone Control, operating on one or both heads (depending on the model) enabling the player to switch—literally in a second—from a normal clear tone to that characteristic indian drum effect and back again at will—a new aid to flashing showmanship.

SPECIFICATIONS: Shells are sturdy, 3-ply laminated construction, beautifully finished in a choice of "Dress Parade" finishes; Hardware is polished chromium plated; hoops are inlaid with Gretsch-Pearl. Heads are tympani-grade transparent calf, fine for tones easily tensioned; the fixed heads on the single-tension models are selected pigskin, finished in white, weather-proof lacquer.

GRETSCH-GLADSTONE SINGLE TENSION
With Single "Finger Tip" Tone Control

Shell	Duco Finishes	Gretsch-Pearl
10"x 6½"	5M8015—$25.50D	5M8020—$30.00D
12"x 8"	5M8016— 31.50D	5M8021— 36.00D
14"x12"	5M8017— 36.50D	5M8022— 42.00D
14"x12"	5M8018— 42.00D	5M8023— 56.00D
16"x10"	5M8019— 50.00D	5M8024— 58.50D

Genuine gold plated metal parts, $3.75D extra

GRETSCH-GLADSTONE SEPARATE TENSION
With Double "Finger Tip" Tone Controls

Shell	Duco Finishes	Gretsch-Pearl
12"x 8"	5M8025—$45.50D	5M8030—$60.00D
14"x12"	5M8026— 50.00D	5M8031— 56.00D
14"x12"	5M8027— 51.00D	5M8032— 56.00D

Genuine gold plated metal parts, $7.50D extra

O'NEIL SPENSER
of John Kirby's Orchestra is a wizard on his
GRETSCH-GLADSTONE Tom Toms.

Gretsch-Gladstone Toms, Author's collection

Curiously, with all this concern over elaborate tensioning, the Gretsch-Gladstone bass drums were single tensioned. Most professional quality bass drums at the time were separate tensioned, including the Gretsch Broadkaster line. Separate tensioning allows the player to tension each head separately to get the optimum tone from the drum. Like the two-way snare drums, the player-side tension rods on the Gretsch-Gladstone bass drums had the decorative two-step tops. Within the lug, it simply screwed into the audience-side tension rod. A spin-on key similar to the three-way key was supplied, but with only one socket. Both heads were equipped with the Gladstone tone controls. August "Gus" Helmecke, bass drummer for the Goldman Band and John Phillip Sousa, also celebrated as the preeminent bass drummer of all time, endorsed the Gretsch-Gladstone bass drum. Gretsch-Gladstone tom toms were equipped with the fingertip tone controls and were offered with either metal or wood hoops and either separate or single tensioned. The single tensioned toms had tacked-on bottom heads, again, odd, with all the concern over tensioning. This tacked-on style was a carryover from the earlier Chinese tom toms that were imported with tacked-on pig skin heads. O'Neil Spenser, drummer for the John Kirby Orchestra, didn't

seem to mind as he is pictured in another Gretsch-Gladstone advertisement with the quote "My Gretsch-Gladstone outfit gives back all the 'JIVE' I put in it"! Jo Jones, celebrated drummer in the "All American Rhythm Section" of the Count Basie Band also played the tacked bottom head toms, but with his characteristic timpani tension rods on top. The Gretsch-Gladstone drum caught the attention of drummers worldwide. Gretsch, in partnership with Billy Gladstone had reinvented the drum. William F. Ludwig, Jr. recalls "I remember...Gretsch

O'Neal Spencer Jive, Author's collection

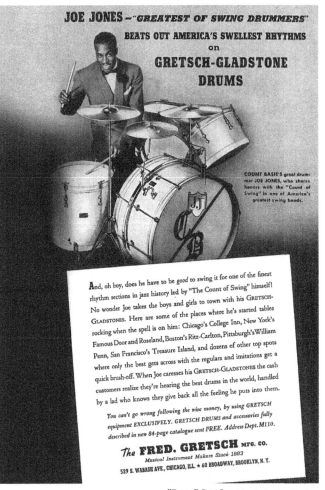

"Papa" Joe Jones, Author's collection

reserving a suite at the Sherman Hotel (in Chicago)...and inviting all the Chicago drummers to see the marvelous Gladstone drum. The drum sold for $100 ($1427 in 2006 dollars), which was ridiculous in those days. Our top of the line drum was $35 ($499 in 2006 dollars)."[23] As ridiculous as it may have seemed, Gretsch-Gladstone drums were being used by prominent drummers of the day.

GRETSCH and GRETSCH-GLADSTONE DRUMS
FIRST CHOICE OF THE GREATEST NAMES IN EVERY FIELD OF MUSIC!

Type of Music	Organization	The Drummer	The Drum
Symphony	Arturo Toscanini's N.B.C. Symphony Orchestra	Dave Grupp	Gretsch-Gladstone
Theatre	Erno Rapee's Radio City Music Hall Symphony Orch.	Wm. D. Gladstone	Gretsch-Gladstone
Concert Band	Dr. Edwin Franko Goldman's Band	Phil Grant Frank Kutak Gus Helmecke	Gretsch-Gladstone
Swing Band	Benny Goodman's Orchestra	Nick Fatool	Gretsch-Gladstone
Swing Band	Count Basie's Orchestra	Joe Jones	Gretsch-Gladstone
Small Combination	Benny Goodman's Sextette	Nick Fatool	Gretsch-Broadkaster
Show Band	Horace Heidt's Musical Knights	Bernie Mattinson	Gretsch-Gladstone
Continental	Xavier Cugat's Orchestra	Alberto Calderon	Gretsch-Gladstone
All-Girl Show Band	Phil Spitalny's All-Girl Orchestra	Mary McClanahan	Gretsch-Gladstone
Feature Band	Bobby Byrne's Orchestra	Sheldon Manne	Gretsch-Gladstone
All-Girl Swing Band	"The Coquettes"	Viola Smith	Gretsch-Broadkaster
"Jump" Band	Al Cooper's Savoy Sultans	"Razz" Mitchell	Gretsch-Broadkaster

Send for your FREE copy of the new 84-page, fully illustrated catalogue of GRETSCH DRUMS. Address Dept. M-81

FRED. GRETSCH MFG. CO.
Drum Makers Since 1883
60 BROADWAY   BROOKLYN, N. Y.

[23] "Reminiscing With William F. Ludwig Jr." by Paul Schmidt, *Modern Drummer,* vol. 11, no. 9, Modern Drummer Publications, Inc., Cedar Grove, NJ, 1989

The paramount endorser among this group was the inimitable "Chick" Webb. Webb's prowess as a big band drummer during the 30's was best summed up by Buddy Rich. "He represents true hippness. His playing was original, different, completely his own...You know, only about a half-dozen of the top

Chick Webb with his Gretsch-Gladstones, Author's collection

drummers since then, including today's so-called 'great' drummers, have anything resembling what he had. If he were alive now, I think most drummers would be running around trying to figure out why they decided to play the drums. That's how good he was!...Gene (Krupa) got to the heart of the matter when he said, after the Goodman-Webb band battle at the Savoy in '37. 'I've never been cut by a better man'...Before the night was over, Gene stood up on Benny's stand and bowed to Chick, as if to say, 'You're the King'".[24] Webb's greatness was achieved in spite of his handicap of being a hunchback, a result of a childhood accident. His pedals, high hat and bass drum, had to be built up so that he could reach them from a normal playing position. Nick Fatool recalls "I first heard Chick Webb in 1932. He was such a little man, hunchbacked, that they had to pick him up and put him on the drums. But once he was set up, he could really play those drums. At the time he was the greatest that I ever heard". ""There were great drummers in those times. But they weren't in the same league as Chick Webb. Compared to him, they were society drummers. You

know what I mean?'–Doc Cheatham. His set was interesting and unusual...it was a console-type kit that moved on wheels...A trap table, including tem-

Nick Fatool, Author's collection

ple blocks, was set right in the center, across a large twenty eight-inch bass drum. Surrounding the table were his snare with wooden rims, made by Billy Gladstone, the great concert drummer, a nine-by-thirteen-inch tom on the bass drum, and another tom–sixteen-by-sixteen-inch (actually sixteen by

Nick Fatool's Gretsch-Gladstone, Author's collection

fourteen)—on the floor. His Zildjian cymbals–a large one on the right, a smaller one on the

24 *Drummin' Men*, by Burt Korall–Schirmer Books, New York, NY, 1990

"King of Drums", Author's collection

left–were hung on loop hangers from goose-neck stands attached to the bass drum".[25] The finish on the drums was striking as well. Covered in white oriental pearl, each drum was also inlayed with contrasting green sparkle "chicks" around the center of the drum. The console, offered in the 1939 Gretsch catalogue, was actually manufac-tured by Premier Drums in England. Gretsch replaced the stock wooden trap table sup-plied by Premier,

Gretsch Drummers' Wheeled Console,
Author's collection

with another Gladstone invention, "a transparent (Plexiglass) trap table which covers the drummers whole outfit but does not conceal it from the audience. Audiences are very curious about drummers and their gadgets. They like to see everything, fascinated by the drummer's equipment and performance".[26]   Webb is prominently pictured on the cover of the 1939 Gretsch catalogue with his "Chick" Gretsch-Gladstone console set.   Sharing the cover is Bernie Mattinson, a drummer also well-known for his technique.   A comparison of the two

Gretsch catalogue offered in the September 1939 *The Metronome*,
Author's collection

drummers is revealing. While Mattinson has the appearance and composure of a "society drummer", the "King of Drums" as Chick Webb was known, appears to be in ecstasy behind his set of Gretsch-Gladstones. With his head rolled back and arms flailing, Chick has all the appearance of "true hippness".

Also featured in this catalogue is another Gladstone invention, the Gretsch-Gladstone hi hat. Similar to the "remote hi hats" of today, this early version clamped on the bass drum hoop and via a flexible cable, was operated by a foot pedal that could be "placed in any position that

[25] IBID

[26] "Gladstone Invents Gadgets While Drumming" *The Metronome*, vol. 53, no. 9 Metronome Publishing Co., New York, NY, 1937

a drummer finds convenient and comfortable".[27] Once again, Billy was ahead of his time. Curiously, yet another Gladstone invention, the "Glass Drum" is not listed in the catalogue though shown by Gretsch at the Music Trades Convention and mentioned in *The Metronome* arti-

Gretsch-Gladstone Hi Hat, Author's collection

cle reporting on the show. "This same material (Lucite) was used by Gladstone to make what looks like a glass drum. This has artistic and entertainment value, by virtue of the lighting effects which may be used inside the transparent drum".[28] I wonder if, decades later, John Bohnam knew the origins of his famous Ludwig Vistalite plexiglass drumset?

Gretsch-Gladstones continued to attract the endorsement of other prominent drummers of the day, including Mary McClanahan of Phil Spitalny's "All-Girl Orchestra", Alberto Calderon with Xavier Cugat's Band, and Shelly Manne.

Billy and his "Glass Drum", Author's collection

Shelly Manne's father, Max Manne arbitrarily chose the saxophone as his young son's musical instrument. Manne recalls, "In addition to being an excellent timpanist, my father was also the contractor of a large orchestra at Radio City Music Hall. I was around musicians all the time. One of these musicians was the great percussionist Billy Gladstone. Billy could see that I was more interested in (jazz) drums than the saxophone. One day, when I was

about 18, Billy and I secretly took my saxophone to Manny's (Music, New York) where we traded it for a set of drums. Billy became my first teacher. The first lesson I ever had was in the percussion room, downstairs, at Radio City Music Hall. Billy showed me how to set up the drums and how to hold the sticks. He put Count Basie's 'Topsie' (with 'Papa' Jo Jones on drums) on the phonograph, told me to play, and then walked out of the room".[29]

Shelly with Stan Kenton, Author's collection

Gladstone was also getting his share of press, including the prestigious cover of *The Metronome* magazine in August of 1938. Billy, practically giving a lesson on his famous grip, gazes proudly at his creation, the Gretsch-Gladstone snare drum. Also note that he is superimposed over the stage and orchestra pit of Radio City Music Hall.

August 1938 *The Metronome*, Author's collection

27 The Fred Gretsch Manufacturing Company catalogue, Brooklyn, NY, 1939

28 "Gladstone Invents Gadgets While Drumming" *The Metronome*, vol. 53, no. 9, Metronome Publishing Co., New York, NY, 1937

29 "Shelly Manne" by Dave Levine, *Modern Drummer*, vol. 5, no. 7, Modern Drummer Publications, Inc., Cedar Grove, NJ, 1989

William D. Gladstone, featured drummer in the Radio City Music Hall Symphony Orchestra, in action with his GRETSCH-GLADSTONE DRUM.

The Drum in the Spotlight

AMERICA'S OLDEST DRUM HOUSE PRESENTS THE WORLD'S FINEST DRUM . . . *Finest* on the written testimony of some of the leading drum artists in the country. *Finest* by reason of three revolutionary improvements developed by William D. Gladstone, featured drummer of Erno Rapee's Radio City Music Hall Symphony Orchestra. *Finest* because it is an outstanding product of the oldest drum house in America.

The plus-performance of the GRETSCH-GLADSTONE DRUM is insured by these three exclusive features:

3-WAY TENSIONING . . . A feature permitting the separate tensioning of batter-head and snare-head, and simultaneous tensioning of both heads without removing drum from the stand.

PERFECTED SNARE-CONTROL . . . A tap of the drum-stick operates the snare-strainer with lightning-like speed and a single easy motion, without changing tempo or losing a beat.

FINGERTIP TONE-REGULATION . . . A finger-lever in the snare-strainer base gives the drummer instant and positive control of release and resumption of overtones and volume.

Many of the foremost artists in the country have experienced a marked improvement in their technique with the help of the GRETSCH-GLADSTONE DRUM. The exclusive features above free the instrument from the effect of temperature and humidity, and insure a brilliant performance under all conditions.

The FRED. **GRETSCH** MFG. CO.

CHICAGO, ILL.   BROOKLYN, N. Y.

Musical Instrument Makers Since 1883

Mail the Coupon Today!

The Fred Gretsch Mfg. Co.   Dept. M-8
529 South Wabash,   60 Broadway,
CHICAGO, ILL.   BROOKLYN, N. Y.

Without cost or obligation tell me all about the GRETSCH-GLADSTONE DRUM and free Trial Plan.

NAME ....

STREET ....

CITY .... STATE.......

In the spotlight, Author's collection

On page 5 of the edition, both Billy and his drum are spotlighted in a Gretsch advertisement. It is no wonder that Billy Gladstone had such an identity with the Music Hall. Ted Reed, writer, educator and close friend of Gladstone wrote "A Tribute to Billy Gladstone" in the October 1981 issue of *Modern Drummer*. "I arrived in New York City in the summer of 1940 with hopes of making my mark in the music business. I heard

Ted Reed's *Progressive Steps to Syncopation*, Author's collection

many things about Billy Gladstone back in Wilkes-Barre, Pennsylvania, so I made a point of catching each new show at Radio City Music Hall, where he was performing. I wanted to hear the great Music Hall orchestra but was especially interested in hearing Billy Gladstone play. The man was a great musician and an absolute perfectionist". Reed was also enamoured with Gladstone's drums. Pictured on the cover of my book *Gretsch Drums, The Legacy Of "That Great Gretsch Sound"* is a seven by fourteen Gretsch-Gladstone finished in gold lacquer with gold plated hardware. Originally owned by Billy Gladstone, the drum was purchased from Ted Reed in 1987. Approximately thirty years earlier Billy told Ted that he had sold the drum to Joe Castka who accompanied Gladstone at the Music Hall. Mr. Reed bought the drum from Castka and restored it to its current condition. Reed continues, "I would arrive at

Billy's Gretsch Gladstone, Author's collection

the start of each stage show and sit at the right side near the percussion section. The pit would come up and the orchestra would play the overture. The orchestra was then lowered a few feet and the stage show would begin. Billy was great at catching the tricks and cues for all the acts. Often, he'd perform a particular trick which I liked and I'd go back to catch the act a second time and he'd play something different–and better! He never stopped trying to improve. He often memorized the shows he had played so many times and at first, musicians who came to see him believed he couldn't read music. Of course this was untrue. Billy was an excellent reader who was not only proficient on snare drum, but on all the percussion instruments as well...conductor Erno Rapee would have no one but Billy".[30]

Phil Grant was the sales manager and artist relations person at Gretsch for many years. Prior to that he was an accom-

Phil Grant (l) with the Goldman Band percussion section, Author's collection

plished snare drummer for the Goldman Band in New York and the Pittsburgh Symphony. "Billy Gladstone was probably the best snare drummer in the country and I was second. I didn't mind being number two to Billy! I used to sub at Radio City Music Hall. They liked me because I had the ability to sight read anything. I could play better than their regular timpanist. There were three percussionists: Billy on snare drum, a bass drum/cymbal player, and a timpanist. The percussion score had all three parts making it easier to follow the cues. Billy was an inventor. I was playing my part and

[30] "A Tribute to Billy Gladstone" by Ted Reed, *Modern Drummer,* vol. 5 no. 7 Modern Drummer Publications, Inc., Cedar Grove, NJ, 1981

I was looking at what he was supposed to be playing, but he's not playing that. He's inventing! I said afterwards 'Hey Billy, you were supposed to be playing this', and he'd say 'Yeah, yeah'". Obviously, the question was not Gladstone's ability to read. He was, after all, an accomplished musician on many instruments besides all the percussion instruments. This guy was so confident in his ability and position with the Radio City Music Hall Orchestra that he didn't feel it necessary to follow the score. And his demanding and discerning conductor, Erno Rapee obviously concurred. Joe Morello "Billy would do his own drum parts. He'd read the music once, then change the whole thing. What he (played) with the orchestra was better than the (composer/arranger) would write". Phil Grant, "One time I was playing and all of a sudden he stopped what he was doing and came over to me and whispered 'You're playing great Phil'. Just stopped playing. I was a great fan of his and I think he was a good fan of mine, too. Billy Gladstone had superb hands. He was a wonderful guy and a brilliant man". Jake Hanna, famous for his work with the Woody Herman Band concurs. "Phil Grant was a great guy and one hell of a legitimate drummer. He loved Billy Gladstone. It's true that he was second only to Billy Gladstone on the snare drum. That's how good he was. (But) Billy Gladstone was the finest snare drummer that ever lived, a supreme artist. He had his own technique. I still try to practice the techniques of Billy. They're awful hard to get down. He was a fine pianist, too; he was just good at everything he did".

The best mechanical description of the Gladstone technique was observed by Ted Reed. "A great deal of Billy's drumming concepts were gathered from his observations of the workings of the piano. The finger system, which he ultimately perfected, came about as a result of careful study of the piano action. One had to study quite some time with Billy to fully understand his technical concepts, but basically the action of the arm, wrist, hand and fingers in Billy's drumming system closely related to the action of the

It's a **GRETSCH**

These 3 Wise Men Know Their Drums!

They're pointing to the GRETSCH nameplate...hall-mark of America's outstanding drums. From left to right, Joe Jones, of Count Basie's Band; "Manny," Boss of New York's foremost rendezvous of professional artists; and Sammy Weiss, whose beat is known wherever radio is heard, are inspecting a GRETSCH key-tension snare drum, in a jive session at "Manny's". They all agree to one thing: "You can't go wrong in picking a drum from the Oldest Drum House in America."

$179.50
PROMPT DELIVERIES

GRETSCH "DEFENDER" DRUM OUTFIT
No big-band drummer ever laid his sticks over this outfit without getting the response he expected, or being enthusiastic in boosting it as the best combination on the market for all-purpose band and orchestra dance-delivery.

Sturdy, fine-toned, finished in 2-tone Blue and Gray shaded lacquer. Shells and hoops made by the exclusive GRETSCH 3-ply laminated process. Perfect round guaranteed. Consists of:

SNARE DRUM separate tension model
BASS DRUM separate tension model
2 Pc. TUNABLE TOM-TOMS each with holder, Trap Rail; Wood Block and Cowbell with combination Holder; Drum Pedal; Tambourine; all-wood, folding Snare Drum Stand; 3 pairs Hickory Sticks; Instruction Book.

GRETSCH-DEFENDER Drum Outfit, complete as described; consult your dealer . . . Each $179.50

The **FRED. GRETSCH** MFG. CO.
Musical Instrument Makers Since 1883
218 S. WABASH AVE., CHICAGO 4, ILL. • 60 BROADWAY, BROOKLYN 11, N.Y.

Gretsch "Defender" drums,
Author's collection

piano key striking the rod, which strikes the hammer, which in turn strikes the string. He believed it was impossible to drum with just the arms and the wrist. He felt the fingers had to be involved. He acquired a great finger technique during his career which enabled him to execute fast, delicate parts with great ease".[31] Gladstone also advised never to go to the maximum of your limits when performing. "Always maintain a reserve that you never use when performing". Practice was another matter. As Phil Grant concurs, "Practice each rudiment very slowly until a firm even beat has been attained. Gradually increase the speed up to the limit of your ability and then slow down to the original speed. Slow diligent practice is the surest way to successful performance. Evenness of beat and sure stick control are more important than speed".

The United States' entry into World War II resulted in an abrupt end in the production of Gretsch-Gladstone drums. By January 1942, President Roosevelt announced that US factories would build 60,000 planes, 45,000 tanks, 20,000 anti-aircraft guns, and 8,000,000 tons of shipping. By 1943 those numbers were met and doubled, outproducing many times the combined arms output of all the Axis powers: Germany, Italy, and Japan. Every effort was channeled toward the defense effort. As a result, the United Stares Government created the War Production Board. The WPB was the regulatory watchdog of all industry, having the implicit power to control all resources and industrial production. Military production came first and as a result, all non-war related manufacturing was limited to 10% metal content by volume. This put a tremendous damper on the nonessential drum industry. Drum companies substituted wood for most metal parts. Slingerland "Rolling Bombers", Ludwig "Victory", WFL "Victorious", Leedy "Dreadnought", and Gretsch "Defender" drums, with wooden lugs and hoops were the result. A drum as mechanically elaborate as the Gretsch-Gladstone was out of the question and was therefore discontinued during the war.

31 IBID

After the war, Gladstone was granted a patent design for another non-musical invention, "A Combination Lighter and Cigarette Case" (number 141,684). Later that year, in the November 1945 *The Metronome,* a full-page advertisement appears announcing "The New Gretsch-Gladstone" with a picture of an out-of-focus drum behind a veiled curtain.

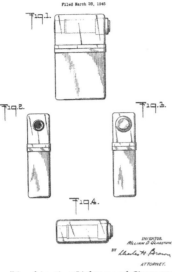

"Combination Lighter and Cigarette Case" patent design drawing, Author's collection

Disappointingly, the first Gretsch catalogue after the war omitted the Gretsch-Gladstone 3-Way Tension drum, opting to offer only the standard 2-Way drum. This catalogue was a Spartan three or four pages, another indication of a lack of direction.

Gladstone was given another professional albeit, personal blow when, in 1945, his long time colleague and good friend Erno Rapee died. Rapee was revered by all the members of the orchestra including Frank Siegfried in the violin section. "I was engaged (September of 1937) as a fiddle player until November of 1942, going into the armed forces. There is no question in my mind that Rapee was a cock-eyed musical and conducting genius. He was a rough, tough little man but GOOD!!! (and also a magnificent pianist)". When Rapee died, the orchestra was assured that their jobs would continue, unchanged. When Charles "Charlie" Previn (Andre Previn's uncle) took over as conductor, this proved to be true. Previn continued as conductor for two years return-

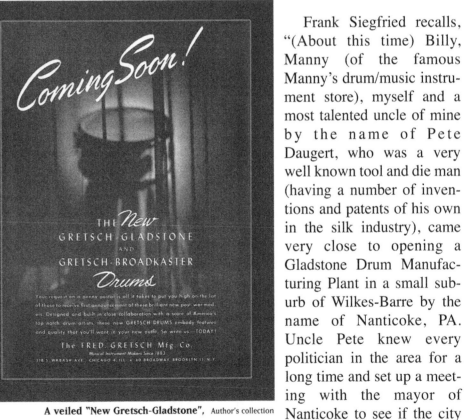

A veiled "New Gretsch-Gladstone", Author's collection

ing to the west coast movie industry. Siegfried continues, "Billy's wife Dorothy and my wife Marjorie worked together as Rockette dancers. We all four felt very close to one another. As a matter of fact, upon being released from service, I did not choose to go back into the Music Hall orchestra and it was (Billy) and dear Dottie that literally talked me into going back in September 1947, when Alexander Smallens was named musical director". Despite all these changes in leadership, the orchestra remained intact, further mitigating Billy's tenure.

Charles Previn,
Courtesy Radio City Music Hall

Alexander Smallens,
Courtesy Radio City Music Hall

Frank Siegfried recalls, "(About this time) Billy, Manny (of the famous Manny's drum/music instrument store), myself and a most talented uncle of mine by the name of Pete Daugert, who was a very well known tool and die man (having a number of inventions and patents of his own in the silk industry), came very close to opening a Gladstone Drum Manufacturing Plant in a small suburb of Wilkes-Barre by the name of Nanticoke, PA. Uncle Pete knew every politician in the area for a long time and set up a meeting with the mayor of Nanticoke to see if the city would be interested in 'sponsoring' a plant of that nature. It so happens that the mayor was a great fan of Billy Gladstone, coming to New York regularly to catch the shows at the Music Hall. Not only would he sponsor such a plan but was honored to do so. We could have the plot of land tax free, he would arrange for the building to be built, we'd be honored at City Hall, etc., etc., etc. However, when it got right down to the nitty gritty, Manny, who was one of Billy's great enthusiasts (and whose business was helped immeasurably by Billy always visiting his store on 48th Street), backed out of the deal. Silently, this was a great disappointment to Billy (and myself of course). It would have been such a 'happy marriage' between Billy and Pete. Billy often said to me 'At last I finally found a guy who really understands manufacturing and production'. Pete had just finished being the top boss of a plant near Wilkes-Barre that manufactured parts for the Grumman Aircraft Company, running the plant on Navy specifications of 'one thousandth of an inch' tolerance. So there was no question that Pete knew what the hell he was doing...and Billy and Pete really would have been a great combination. Sad that it did not happen because, I think, it would have been enormously successful, what with the Gladstone name and fame connected with the musical product".

In 1949 Gladstone was granted three patents for wire brushes. The first ("Drum Beater" number 2,485,822) was Billy's adaptation of the popular version of the wire brush. In the treatise, he notes that the metal rod protruding from the rear of the brush can be used to control the spread of the wires of the brush. He maintains that this change in rod length alters the balance of the brush and the rod adjustment can inadvertently change during usage of the brush. His design overcame these drawbacks by placing threads on the rod nearest the brush wires to permit adjustment of the wire brush spread.

"Drum Beater" patent drawing,
Author's collection

"Drum Beater" patent drawing,
Author's collection

On the opposite end the handle is a groove which locks the rod in place after the adjustment has been made. The second patent ("Drum Beater" number 2,485,823) is a variation on the above, with the adjustment made on the opposite end of the control rod (furthest from the brush wires). For the hoop-end style, he proposed a spiral spring on the hoop end which can be extended to control the wire brush spread. For the ball-end type brush, he proposed a threaded shaft on the rod furthest from the brush wires with the ball serving as the adjustment knob. A set screw in the ball prevents changes in adjustment while playing. Finally, ("Drum Beater" number 2,485,824) is a double ended brush with each end having different apertures varying the wire brush spread. The summer of 1950, Billy was granted a patent ("Drum Beater" number 2,513,930) for yet another variation on the wire brush design. Here, the hoop end of the control rod had a fastening element that aligned with corresponding holes in the handle to permit control of the wire brush spread.

Billy Gladstone's disappointment over the failure of the Gladstone Drum Factory was only

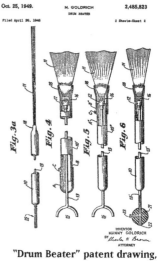

"Drum Beater" patent drawing,
Author's collection

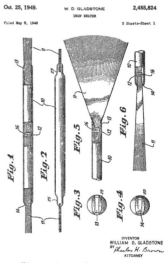

"Drum Beater" patent drawing,
Author's collection

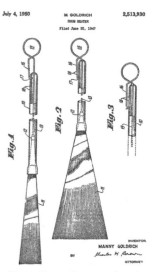

"Drum Beater" patent drawing,
Author's collection

the beginning of his problems. Arthur Press, "In 1951, (actually September 1950) Raymond Paige got the job as Music Director/Conductor at Radio City Music Hall. He decided that he was going to release, fire, non-renewal, whatever word you want to call it, all the older crew in the (Music Hall) orchestra which was about ninety-five percent.

Raymond Paige,
Courtesy Radio City Music Hall

Apparently, he wanted to be associated with only very young people and you certainly had to have hair. Billy, of course, had hair, but (Paige) just threw the whole bunch out which was really unfortunate. The Musician's Union should have stepped-in and said 'What the hell are you doing'? Billy left the Music Hall a very bitter man. He felt it was unjustified, especially when he saw other guys come in...guys like (Harold) Farberman, who was a wonderful player, but relaxed, and took the Hall in proper perspective. It was only a job and you played it the best you can. Billy thought the Music Hall was his job forever and had an identity with it that you wouldn't believe. As a matter of fact, he had a picture of the Music Hall Orchestra with his own picture superimposed right over the top of the stage (probably the artwork for the August 1938 *The Metronome)*. He felt such an affinity toward the job. I saw that (picture) hanging in his apartment. My own career at the Music Hall started in 1952 as a substitute player for Farberman and Al Howard". Frank Siegfried concurs "I was there when the 'Paige Purge' took place that Arthur Press accurately describes. The entire New York City music community was shocked when Raymond Paige fired Billy Gladstone. I somehow survived the 'Paige Purge' (how or why I will never know to this day). Paige let me suffer under his baton

Gladstone (top right) just before the"Page Purge", Courtesy Radio City Music Hall

(but) I was purged in his second year. I remember both Arthur Press and Harold Farberman very well and albeit they were talented 'kids', neither of them had the right to stand in Billy Gladstone's footprints in the pit of the Radio City Music Hall at that time.

They have both since carved very successful careers for themselves–and deservedly so. After all, we're talking about 47 years here and one can learn a heluva lot in 47 years if he/she puts their mind to it". Ted Reed, "Paige let all of the excellent orchestra players go, replacing them with younger musicians. The quality was gone. The orchestra was never the same".[32]

Billy Gladstone's attitude toward the inventing process quoted earlier, "I never gave up, I kept plugging, trying" also permeated his whole life. Though bitter about his termination from the Music Hall, he directed his attention toward his budding drum business. After the failed attempt to incorporate a drum factory in Pennsylvania, Billy decided to build custom snare drums in his apartment on 54th Street and 6th Avenue. Keep in mind, custom drums were almost nonexistent at that time, unlike today, where

Billy's personal 7 by 14 Gladstone Custom Drum and stand,
Courtesy Ted Reed

there is a plethora of custom drum manufacturers. As Arthur Press points out, "He was making drums back in the 50's that are the benchmark of what a custom should be...even by today's standards". Billy made his drums in two size configurations, six by fourteen for drumset players and seven by fourteen for concert/symphonic players. According to Arthur Press, Billy thought that the seven by fourteen mathematical combination would be best. Press continues "He hated pearl coverings. Billy said 'They use pearl on toilet seats. If you want a toilet seat buy a Ludwig or a Gretsch drum'". Gladstone did make some six by fourteen with pearl coverings but only at the ardent demand of the owner. His preferred finishes were black, white or gold lacquer, or clear lacquer over a birdseye maple shell. Joe Morello's request for a

32 IBID

Gladstone drum was spurned for this very reason, "When I took my first lesson in 1954, he (Gladstone) wanted to make me one, but I wanted it in silver (sparkle) pearl. That was my trademark. Billy said 'Oh, I can't do that. I don't want to put plastic on the drum.' He wanted to make a drum in black lacquer but I wanted something to match the drumset. So that was it, no animosity, he just didn't believe in anything covering the drum". I noted that Gladstone did make some drums with pearl coverings. Morello responded "Well, he didn't do it for me! If I had bugged him long enough maybe he would have". Ted Reed explains Gladstone's disdain for pearl coverings, "Billy liked wood shells and would often say 'They don't put pearl on violins do they? It would kill the sound'. The insides of his drum shells were finished (lacquered) just as smoothly as the outside

Gladstone drum interior, Author's collection

which he felt was extremely important in obtaining a good sound. He also used thin flesh hoops (the hoop that the drumhead is mounted onto) which floated and did not touch the shell. He was a firm believer in 'the less that touched the shell, the better the sound would be'" [33]

Arthur Press continues, "He was also concerned about the drum being stifled by die-cast lugs (commonly used by drum manufacturers at that time). The best lug he could imitate was the old Ludwig post lug with a small fitting that contacted the shell". Gladstone used either hex head machine screws or pan head screws to attach the lugs to the drum. Press continues, "Of course you are familiar with that marvelous three-way tuning system he designed".

It should be noted that Gladstone reverted back to his original patent design for his custom drums, uti-

Gladstone drum post lug, Author's collection

lizing a hex shaft and socket differential for his tension rods. As with the Gretsch-Gladstone, the three-way key was mounted on a threaded shaft on the side of the drum. Inscribed on the key were a Billy Gladstone script logo and the two patent numbers for

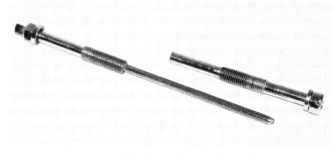

Gladstone drum tension rods, Author's collection

the three-way design. Behind the key was a triangular badge bearing the same information as the key. "Billy designed the key and badge so that when the

Inscribed Gladstone key and badge, Author's collection

key was spun on the drum, the Billy Gladstone logo on the key lined up with the same logo on the badge", Arthur Press. Gladstone's throw-off (over-center) was similar to the Gretsch-Gladstone, but worked more efficiently and designed with much less mass. Press continues, "His throw-off was designed so he could play and throw the snares off (or on) with a flick of the stick without having to use his hand. The internal muffler had a numbered scale on the outside so he could return the muffler to a previously desired setting. Of course numbers didn't matter, but he just loved that kind of concept. Everything was just so pristine about his drums". Unlike the spring-loaded tone control of the

Gladstone throw-off with built-in tone control, Author's collection

Gretsch-Gladstone, Billy's new design utilized a worm gear mechanism (actually a string tuning mechanism from a guitar) so the muffler could be applied gradually yet quickly. The muffler was part of the throw off mechanism. Ted Reed told me Billy not only perfected throwing on or off the snares with a stick in his left hand while rolling with his right, but at the same time, adjusting the tone control with the pinkie finger of his left

Billy demonstrating his throw off and tone control single-handedly to Ted Reed, Courtesy Ted Reed

hand. Talk about finger control! The receiving end of the snares (the butt plate) was similar to the butt of the gut snare-equipped Gretsch-Gladstone drums. In the same manner, the gut passed through a metal block with tension screws to hold each pair of gut strands in place. "What cannot be seen from the

Internal Gladstone tone control, Author's collection

outside, and is an indication of the care lavished on this instrument, is a small leather disc between the set screw and the gut strand. This prevents the gut from being damaged by the tension of the set screw (or) indenting

Original Gladstone butt plate, Author's collection

the gut. The indentation might cause the strand to pop back to its former position when an adjustment is made. The original design was a one piece casting that held eight strands, and a small bar (pinch plate) attached with screws machined with a head that fit the square (socket) on the three-way key. The (bar) had openings for four more strands. At a lesson back in 1952, Gladstone told Arthur Press that he had seen a beautiful ankle bracelet in the window of an exclusive Fifth Avenue shop and was going to use the design for a new butt end. The design was used, starting with the drum made for Arthur Press. The small knob above the butt is ingenious

Second generation Gladstone butt plate, Author's collection

in that it houses a hex key that fits the set screws holding the strands of gut. The six 1/8" holes (surrounding the key) go through the shell and are air holes. Another air hole is built into the throw-off. Billy did not like the air hole showing, so they were built into the design of the drum".[34] Billy approached wire snares with an interesting idea. In an effort to utilize

Gladstone hex tool and mounting bracket with air holes, Author's collection

the existing clamping mechanisms and therefore, controlling the tension of each individual snare wire,

34 "Tech-Talk: The Gladstone Butt End" by Morris "Arnie" Lang, *Gladstone Society Newsletter,* vol 2 no. 1, Lang Percussion Inc. Publication, Brooklyn, NY, 1997

Billy inserted the wire snares into pieces of electrical wire insulation and glued them into place. Unlike the plastic wire insulation of today, the old style was rigid and performed like a piece of gut. Gladstone even used wire insulation the color of gut. Hardware was either plated in chrome or, upon request, gold. If the drum had gold-plated hardware, Billy even plated the individual snare wires in gold. As Arthur Press says "Everything was just so pristine about his drums".

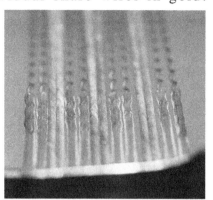

Snares of Arthur Press' Gladstone drum. *He requested a combination of wire and gut,* Author's collection

Another quote, noted earlier in Bill's philosophy on patents, also applied to other aspects of his life, "Business is business". Despite Gretsch's abandonment of the Gretsch-Gladstone 3-way drum after the war, Gladstone maintained a business relationship with the factory. Billy liked Gretsch's early die cast hoops and supplied his custom drums with the same. He also believed in Gretsch's philosophy on shell design. Most drum companies were using plied wood in their shell construction, including Gretsch. The difference is, other manufacturers steam-bent plywood into a circle. As such, all the plies met at one joint or "scarf". Some companies even bent plywood already covered in pearl. Thus, the pearl runs through the joining scarf. This type of shell required reinforcement rings at the top and bottom to keep them in-round. Bill Hagner, plant manager at the Gretsch factory explains, "When I first went to work with Gretsch, November 18, 1941, they were not making drums with reinforcing rings. They bought all the veneers, 1/16 inch maple on the inside and outside plies and an inner ply of 1/8 inch poplar. These plies were cross-grained and glued together. The poplar center ply

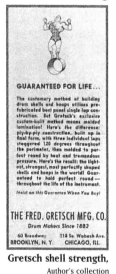

GUARANTEED FOR LIFE...

The customary method of building drum shells and hoops utilizes pre-fabricated bent panel single lap construction. But Gretsch's exclusive custom-built method means molded lamination! Here's the difference: ply-by-ply construction, built up in final form, with three individual laps staggered 120 degrees throughout the perimeter, then molded to perfect round by heat and tremendous pressure. Here's the result: the lightest, strongest, most perfectly shaped shells and hoops in the world! Guaranteed to hold perfect round — throughout the life of the instrument. Insist on this Guarantee When You Buy!

THE FRED. GRETSCH MFG. CO.
Drum Makers Since 1883
60 Broadway   218 So. Wabash Ave.
BROOKLYN, N.Y.   CHICAGO, ILL.

Gretsch shell strength, Author's collection

was used for two reasons: one, it made the drum light, second, it was cheap". Gretsch was laminating the wood as they molded the shell. The plies were joined at three different places resulting in a stronger shell that did not require reinforcement rings. The people at the Gretsch felt glue rings "broke up" the sound waves inside the drum. This new process produced a shell that was completely smooth on the inside. Also, the bearing edge that the drumhead rested on was much thinner.

Shell lamination at Gretsch factory, Author's collection

Billy Gladstone was impressed with these features. According to Charles Cordes, Billy's drum mechanic "Billy strongly believed a drum was a lot like a violin. So much so that he didn't believe in putting the reinforcement in the top (bearing edge)".[35] Billy saw the bearing edge like the bridge of a violin. The thinner, the better. Considering the thickness of a bearing edge composed of the shell and a reinforcement ring, it is no wonder Gladstone preferred Gretsch shells.

Shell edges being trimmed at Gretsch factory, Author's collection

Bill Hagner recalls "When Billy went out on his own to build drums I would make the shells for him just the way he wanted. He was extremely particular in any of the merchandise he used. When he put his name on a drum he wanted it to be perfect. His dimensions for where he put the hardware on the drum had to be exact spacing. Otherwise, he thought it would distort the sound. His shells were finished on both the outside and the inside. Billy never used the 4-ply or 6-ply shells we later developed because he thought they were too heavy". For

Drum assembly at Gretsch factory, Author's collection

---

35 "Billy Remembered" *Modern Drummer,* vol. 5 no. 7, Modern Drummer Publications, Inc., Cedar Grove, NJ, 1981

the same weight reasons, Gladstone also continued with the original Gretsch "stick chopper" die-cast rims, even after Gretsch developed the triple flange style. Some of his drums that exist today have the later Gretsch triple flange rims, but they were replacements by a previous owner.

Spray paint booths at Gretsch factory, Author's collection

The first contract that Gladstone received to build a custom drum was from Elden C. "Buster" Bailey. "I was with the New York Philharmonic and Billy and I discussed the possibility of him making me a drum. As a symphonic player I opted for the seven by fourteen inch size drum in black lacquer with gut snares. I received the drum in 1949 and Billy had a special nameplate engraved 'Elden C. Bailey Philharmonic Orchestra New York October 1949 Drum No. 0'. When I asked him why he used the number 0, he explained that he had already started on Shelly Manne's drum but finished mine first. Since Manne's drum was inscribed No. 1, he numbered mine 0. It is a wonderful drum". To identify his drums as custom made, Gladstone placed a small engraved plaque on the shell of the drum between the throw-off and the key, with information about the drum and its owner. Sometimes this inscription included an expression of personal sentiment ("To My Pal Joe Sinai", etc). Shelly Manne's drum

Shelly Manne's Gladstone drum, Courtesy Larry Bunker

was the first six by fourteen inch drum. The plaque is engraved "To Shelly Manne With Admiration Billy Gladstone April 9, 1950 Drum No. 1". Like Bailey's drum, Shelly's drum is finished in black lacquer, but the hardware is plated in gold, making for a stunning looking drum. Before Shelly Manne died (1984), he loaned

the drum to the late LA session drummer Larry Bunker. Bunker was also the percussionist for the Academy Awards orchestra for many years, as well as playing with the likes of Stan

"With Admiration Drum No. 1", Courtesy Larry Bunker

Getz, Art Pepper, Gerry Mulligan and Barney Kessel. Larry always admired the Manne's Gladstone drum and used it several times in his session work. I received a letter from Bunker in 1993 that included the above photos and "In re-reading your article (about Billy Gladstone drums) in *Not So Modern Drummer*, I realized I had erred when I reassembled the drum (I may have done that when I first restored it in '69 or '70). I obviously didn't pay attention to where the key and name badge went and stuck them in the holes that felt right. I'll get the drum home shortly and pull the top head and swap them and get them in their proper places". He continues "I feel Billy's design for the hex shaft (of the top tension rod) was more elegant than the Gretsch (Gladstone) version, in theory, and in appearance. However, I feel that there is an inherent weakness in the design, in that the only thing that holds the top tension rod assembly together is the small lip that is rolled onto the crown of the top rod. Two of those had been damaged on the (Manne) drum. The hex shaft would bind in the bottom (tension) rod socket, and

Design problem, Courtesy Larry Bunker

when the bottom rod was tightened (it would) pull the hex shaft up through the lip. I was able to persuade Dominic Calicchio, a trumpet maker, to repair those for me. I keep a thin coat of Vaseline on the hex shaft/socket juncture, but even so, whenever I have to adjust the bottom head, I always loosen it a pinch first before tightening. Perhaps Billy modified that in later drums (for the record, he didn't). In any event, that shouldn't have been a problem in the Gretsch version because of the small 'D' ring below the top rod that held the blade in place". Another inherent weakness in the design of the top rod was Billy attachment of the square head to the hex shaft. In time, with use, the connection between these two elements would strip, making the tension of the bottom rod impossible. Several of my Gladstone drums had this problem which I remedied by having a machinist insert a spring steel pin through the square head and hex shaft. When Bunker restored Manne drum the original insulation holding the wire snares had to be replaced. Remarkably, Larry found the original style of insulation but only in black. He was kind enough to share his find when I restored one of my snares.

Billy's personal drum was not dated or numbered. The plaque simply stated "Billy Gladstone Radio City Music Hall". In mid 80's Ted Reed sent me photo's of his collection of seven Billy Gladstone snares and two Gretsch-Gladstones. Two of the drums were originally owned by Billy, a gold Gretsch-Gladstone and the gold seven by fourteen custom Gladstone snare that Billy used at Radio City Music Hall in the early 50's (prior to the "Page Purge") and all throughout the remainder of his career. Reed noted, "In 1955 Billy gave me the gold snare drum stand he used for so many years at the Music Hall". Along with the photos, Ted sent a typed description of his collection. At the time, my Gladstone collection consisted of only a Billy Gladstone practice pad manufactured by Ludwig, that I used for many years. I eagerly asked if he would be interested in selling any of his drums. His response was a terse, "Nothing that I have that was made by Billy Gladstone is for sale". He continued "When Billy was on the road with the show *My Fair Lady* -1957 to Aug. 1961- he wrote to me several times a week-

Ted Reed's collection of Gladstone drums, Courtesy Ted Reed

Reed's typed description of his Gladstone drum collection, Courtesy Ted Reed

also sent me several gifts. In one letter he had written down the 50 names of the drummers that he made his custom drums for and asked me to type the list and return it to him. I typed it and did not make a copy for myself. However, I did remember some of the names. I do not remember all fifty. I do know about 12 and they will not part with the drum. If they do I will get it. I will buy every B.G. drum I can. I suggest you keep looking-maybe you will come across one before I do". He continued, "I helped Tama Drum Co. develop and make a Gladstone type snare drum. It is a great drum. They sent me one of the custom made drums in Sept. The plate on the drum reads, 'This custom made snare drum is presented with our deepest appreciation to Ted Reed'. It is 6$\frac{1}{2}$ X 14 maple (and)

Tama's presentation Gladstone-type drum, Courtesy Ted Reed

has the Billy Gladstone tuning device-both heads are adjusted from the top. Play on one of them-you will like it. I'll enclose a photo". Ted's offer for a substitution didn't interest me...I wanted a real

Gladstone (or Gretsch-Gladstone) drum. Disappointed, I set my collector eyes in other directions with little hope, as Ted had made a conscious effort to track down the original, what he thought, 50 Gladstone drums. Nevertheless, I continued to correspond with Ted. In subsequent letters he told me that much of the rest

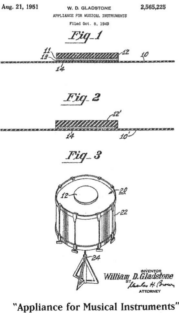

Gladstone key case, Author's collection

of his non-drum Gladstone collection consisted of items Billy had sent him as gifts, an original Gladstone practice pad (pre Ludwig), Gretsch-Gladstone mallets, Hand Sock Cymbals, key cases and Billy's original patent for the Double Action Bass drum pedal. I, in turn, sent Ted copies of the Gladstone patents that I had received from the US Patent Office. Ted already had many of the patents. I also sent a copy of my 1939 Gretsch catalogue that included the Gretsch-Gladstone. Later, Ted sent me two Gladstone key cases as a gift. They are still being produced today. He wrote "I think you will like them. Nothing like it

on the market". In another letter, he told me "In 1959 Billy offered to sell me the patent rights to his pad ("Appliance for Musical Instruments" number 2,565,225 granted in 1951) for $1000.00 ($6814 in 2006 dollars). He also offered to sell me the patent rights to his vibe mallets ("Hammer for Per-cussion Instruments" number 2,853,912, granted in

"Appliance for Musical Instruments" patent drawing, Author's collection

1958) for $1000.00. I was busy playing, teaching and promoting my books and did not have time to devote to getting it fully on the market. William F. Ludwig, Jr. bought the pad. Much better rubber in Billy's. In 1963 I had the chance to buy boxes of Billy Gladstone parts for $2000.00 ($12,960 in 2006 dollars). I turned it down. Jack Adams Drum Shop in Boston bought them".

Gladstone was also trying to sell his patent rights to some of his other inventions. Besides offering the Billy Gladstone Practice Pad to Ted Reed, Billy also offered the pad to George L. Stone (the "son" of George B. Stone & Son, Inc.) in Boston, MA. In an October 1954 letter, George L. responds:

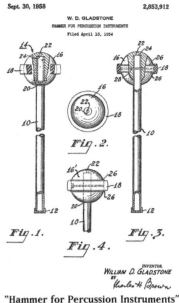

"Hammer for Percussion Instruments" patent drawing, Author's collection

Dear Billy:

Many thanks for the Vacuum Practice Pad you so thoughtfully mailed to me at my home.

The pad is, in my estimation, the finest accessory of its kind that I have ever seen. I think that when drummers have had a chance to see and try it out, you will do very well with it. Brilliant idea.

I suggest you mail a couple of these pads to the firm, via parcel post, together with your invoice for same. I will do my best to get the local boys interested.
My best to you and I am,

Sincerely,
George L. Pres.

Original Billy Gladstone Practice Pad, Author's collection

The Gladstone pad was (and still is) truly unique. The brochure Billy used to promote the item details the features.

Pure gum rubber, eternally resilient. Never hardens, never cracks, never softens; never shows stick marks; gives crisp, live natural drum rebound that develops the reflexes as no other practice pad possibly can.

Molded with patented steel plate imbedded to make an integral structure.

Guaranteed for 10 years.

Patented structure establishes vacuum, holding pad firmly on a drum head, table, chair of any convenient flat surface.

Especially desirable for the professional drummer because it fits right over the batter head of his drum (cannot injure the head but instead is actual protection).

Used on drum, makes ideal practice condition because

1-Faint snare response gives realistic "feel" without undue volume of noise. Fine for warming up right on the band stand.

2-Two playing surfaces with different levels of sound afford perfect medium for timbale and tomtom practice when used with snares thrown off.

3-Being set in the drum the player gets rim shot practice at the same time-ideal for South American rhythms impossible with other practice pads.

4-The variation in sound level between the center pad and the outer cushion provides realistic condition for combination drum, tom tom and cymbal technique.

Pad stays right on the drum for easy carrying.

Not only a practice pad but a usable and useful accessory for actual playing-as in recording, broadcasting and symphonic work where extreme pianissimo is required. Gives adequate volume, audible snare response, perfect control.

Developed by Billy Gladstone who was formally the featured drummer for eighteen years in the Radio City Music Hall Symphony Orchestra, New York City.

take a tip from ☆
☆ the Stars...

BILLY GLADSTONE
World-famous artist with the Radio City Music Hall Symphony, and creative genius with 15 U. S. Patents to his credit, including his masterpiece— the GLADSTONE Drum.

BILLY GLADSTONE'S
Vacuum Drum Pad

Pure gum rubber, eternally resilient. Never hardens, never cracks, never softens; never shows stick marks; gives crisp, live natural drum rebound that develops the reflexes as no other practice pad possibly can.

Moulded with patented steel plate imbedded to make an integral structure.

Guaranteed for 10 years.

Patented structure establishes vacuum, holding pad firmly on drum head, table, chair or any convenient flat surface.

Especially desirable for the professional drummer because it fits right over the batter head of his drum (can not injure the head but instead is actual protection).

Used on drum, makes ideal practice condition because

1—Faint snare response gives realistic tonal "feel" without undue volume of noise. Fine for warming up right on the band stand.

2—Two playing surfaces with different levels of sound afford perfect medium for timbale and tomtom practice when used with snares thrown off.

3—Being set in the drum the player gets rim shot practice at the same time — ideal for South American rhythms impossible with other practice pads.

4—The variation in sound level between the central pad and outer cushion provides realistic condition for combination drum, tom tom and cymbal technique.

Pad stays right on the drum for easy carrying.

Not only a practice pad but a usable and useful accessory for actual playing — as in recording, broadcasting and symphonic work where extreme pianissimo is required. Gives adequate volume, audible snare response, perfect control.

Developed by Billy Gladstone who was formerly the featured drummer for eighteen years in the Radio City Music Hall Symphony Orchestra, New York City.

List 12.50

Original Billy Gladstone Practice Pad brochure, Author's collection

As Reed notes, Ludwig accepted Gladstone's offer to sell the patent right to the pad (in 1959), however for

Ludwig Billy Gladstone Practice Pad, Author's collection

a short time it was sold by Slingerland as the "Buddy Rich Practice Pad". It is unknown if this was a patent infringement. Ludwig was, however, not interested in

Slingerland "Buddy Rich" Practice Pad, Author's collection

the Gladstone brushes. In a September 1954 letter, Wm. F. Ludwig, Jr. rejected Gladstone's offer to sell the patent rights to his brushes.

Dear Bill:

Thanks a lot for your letter of September 15th, telling us about the new jazz brush and thank you also for the sample which I have received.

Upon looking it over and examining it very carefully, I feel that the price of such an item would be too high for the benefit derived. Most drummers do not adjust their brushes at all and those that do, simply tape them or bend the handle a little which accomplishes the same thing as your device.

Frankly, we have made many models similar to yours, including running a slot down the handle with notches in it and discarded all of these thoughts because of the increased production costs.

Thank you anyway for sending it and we will return it.

Very truly yours,
Bill

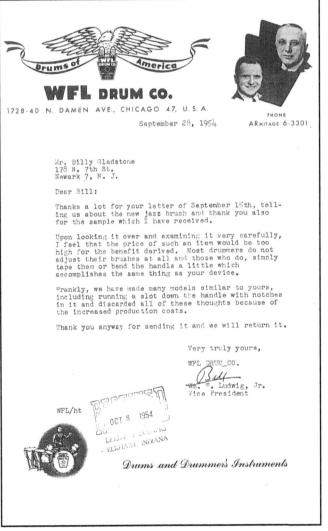

September 28, 1954 Wm. F. Ludwig, Jr. letter to Billy Gladstone, Author's collection

Ludwig's rejection letter prompted a response from Gladstone to his friend and colleague, George Way.

October 6, 1954 Billy Gladstone letter to George Way,
Author's collection

Dear George:

I always said you're tops.

It seems to me that old man Bill Ludwig and my old pal George Way are the only ones that know anything about the drum profession.

Enclosed within is a letter from Wm. F. Ludwig Jr. How about that?

They will go to work and spend money on a cardboard box and charge more for the wire brushes, of which, a drummer has no more use for it than the man on the moon.

At present I am manufacturing the B.G. custom made drums and have sold them to practically all the major symphony organizations throughout the U.S.A.

Here is a list of the orchestras.

N.Y. Philharmonic	Eden C. Bailey
Philadelphia Orch.	Michael Bookspan
Boston Symp.	Harold Farberman
Boston Pops "	Donald Bush
N.B.C. Symp. "	Harry Stitman
Radio City Music Hall Symp.	Arthur Press
Pittsburgh Symp.	Wayne H. Pascuzzi
New Orleans "	
Cincinnati Symp. Orch.	Glenn Robinson
San Francisco "	Joe Sinai
Corpus Christi Texas Sym.	Hal Wasson
Civic Symp. Of Jamestown N.Y	S. H. Skinner
Ballet Theatre	Stanley Koor
Civic Center Ballet	Arnold Lang
Sadler Wells	Arnold Goldberg
Phil Spitalny Girl Orch.	Viola Smith
U.S. Army Band of Wash. D.C	Kane-Battista-Zipp
South Pacific Musical	Dave Gusikoff
Fred Warring Show on Tour	Leslie Parks
Kate Smith T.V. Show	Marty Grupp
Stan Kenton	Shelly Manne
Louis Armstrong	Cozy Cole
Benny Goodman	Morey Feld

Morey Feld who has been playing right along with Benny Goodman is now using a complete set of mine that is really out of this world. He is nuts about his new outfit and so is Benny.

John Noonan wrote me a letter that he recognized the outfit in the Down Beat magazine a few weeks ago and by the way he bought two of my snare drums.

Doing very well with the "Velvet Touch" vibe, bell, glock, and xylophone mallets including a prac-

tice 1¹/₂in. sponge rubber ball.

Also doing terrific with the "Vacuum Practice Drum Pad".

My wife's mother left us a 3 story brick 10 room house and if ever in town stop over, it would be a pleasure to have you stay with us.

With my best,

Billy

Obviously frustrated with Ludwig's rejection, Gladstone nonetheless is enthusiastic about the success of his drum line. Gladstone's zeal for building drums is remembered by Arnold Goldberg of the New York City Ballet Orchestra. "I recall after we decided that the configuration of the drum was a six inch depth birdseye maple shell with gut snares, Billy enthusiastically began assembling the drum. He called me several times, at all hours, to give me a progress report. I remember once, him calling me at 1:00AM, just to tell me that he had treated the gut snares and they were hanging to dry. That passion permeated every part of Billy's life, especially his performance on stage. His incredible technique was punctuated by grandiose body movements, high sticking, head movements, even the way he held his jaw. What a performance"! [36]

I don't know if I wore Ted Reed down, or it was simply my enthusiasm, but in August of 1987 I received a most surprising letter. "I have decided to let you buy the gold Gretsch-Gladstone drum. The price is $250. Billy used the drum in Radio City Music Hall until he made his own drums. Then he sold it to Joe Castka, one of the other drummers in the Music Hall. I bought it from Joe Castka. I hope you enjoy owning it as much as I did". As you can imagine,

JOSEPH CASTKA of the Percussion Section of Erno Rapee's Radio City Music Hall Symphony Orchestra, New York, is pictured here with the giant K. Zildjian Cymbals used by this famous orchestra. Mr. Castka's brilliant technique and showmanship on cymbals and Bass Drum is a never-failing delight to Music Hall audiences.

Joe Castka, Author's collection

I couldn't get to the post office fast enough. After I received the drum I changed the Gretsch wire snares attached to the drum to varnished gut, as I thought that is how Billy would have it. I advised Ted of my alteration and his response was "Glad to hear you were able to fix the Gretsch-Gladstone to your liking, but Billy used shellac on the gut snares-not varnish. It is a beautiful drum-enjoy it"! I since changed the drum back to the way Ted shipped it to me. Ted recants the story of his custom Gladstone drum. "I opened my drum studio on 47th Street in February of 1954 and Billy was a frequent visitor. I talked him into making me a snare drum. The price was $250 ($1843 in 2006 dollars) and I asked him to cover it with white pearl but he flatly refused claiming, 'they put pearl on toilet seats'.

Billy's Gretsch-Gladstone with Gladstone-type stand, Author's collec-

I decided on birdseye maple and Billy delivered the drum at Christmastime of '54. The drum and (Gladstone's) stand are both pictured on the cover of my book *Progressive Steps to Syncopation*. It made Billy very happy. I can clearly remember how Billy went to pieces when Dorothy passed away September of that year. He wouldn't eat and he wouldn't play. I finally got him to do both after a great deal of persuasion. Shortly after Dorothy's death, Billy sold his home and moved into a one room apartment on West 48th

Ted Reed's Gladstone drum and stand, Courtesy Ted Reed

36 "Billy Gladstone Custom Drums" by Chet Falzerano, *Percussive Notes,* vol. 32 no. 4, Percussive Arts Society, Lawton, OK, 1994

Street, an apartment he never let me see always claiming, 'It's too messed up'".[37] The house that "Billy sold" was the one mentioned in Gladstone's letter to George Way. It was located on 7th Street in Newport, NJ. Gladstone's suffering over the loss of his wife is also remembered by Joe Morello, "I met Billy in 1954 when he came to see me at the Hickory House (in New York). I talked to him about taking lessons. At first he didn't want to teach me. He said, 'You and Buddy Rich, you don't need this'. I said 'But I really want to take some lessons from you'. It was unfortunate because his wife had just passed away so all during the lesson he was crying and telling me how much he loved his wife. That was my first lesson".

My next Gladstone drum came to me by way of *Modern Drummer* magazine. In the September 1984 issue, one of the feature articles is "Arthur Press, Classical Wisdom". Along with noting Press' illustrious career with the Radio City Music Hall Orchestra and the Boston Symphony Orchestra, they discussed the tools of his trade including his Billy

Arthur Press' Gladstone drum, Author's collection

Gladstone custom snare drum. He liked the drum for "those dark Mahler passages". I was beginning to think my Gladstone collection was going to be easy because when I called Press, he immediately agreed to sell me his drum. We settled on a price and once again I rushed off to the post office. Five days later I received a letter from Press, "While I was packing up the drum I decided I just can't part with it. I am returning your check". Though I totally understood

his sentiment, as frankly, I couldn't believe he would sell such a keepsake, I was also understandably very disappointed. One year later I get another letter, "I'm ready". Though dubious, I sent out another check. Five days later it arrived. A few weeks later, I received an audio cassette with Press' recollections of the drum and his experiences with Billy Gladstone. I also had the pleasure of visiting with Arthur when the Boston Symphony appeared in San Francisco. In Press' audio tape description he notes, "Harold Farberman left me his (Gladstone) drum when I subbed for him at Radio City Music Hall. When Farberman left to go to the Boston Symphony I got the job in 1952 as solo percussionist at the Music Hall. Knowing I need a snare drum and after having played on Farberman's Gladstone, I thought it was time for me to get a Gladstone drum.

The author, Arthur Press and his Gladstone drum, Author's collection

I contacted Billy and he said, 'Why don't you come over to the apartment. I have a few drums I could show you'. He lived in an apartment house on 54th Street and 6th Avenue. When I got there he had a birdseye maple drum and a black lacquer drum. I chose the black drum. To this day I think the black snare drum has the most dress appearance, like a grand piano being rolled out onto the stage...a wonderful formal look that I think is gorgeous. I used the drum at the Music Hall. I then went to the Boston symphony in 1956 as the bass drummer and utility percussionist. When Harold Farberman left the symphony in 1960, I became the principal snare drummer. I used the drum whenever I was required to play dark passages like Mahler symphonies, and the 'Bartok Sonata for Two Piano and Percussion', as the drum has a dark quality". Though we did not have enough time for Arthur to give me a lesson on

37 "A Tribute to Billy Gladstone" by Ted Reed, *Modern Drummer*, vol. 5 no. 7, Modern Drummer Publications, Inc., Cedar Grove, NJ, 1981

the Gladstone finger technique, he did demonstrate what he learned from Billy on his Gladstone drum. Though I do not feel qualified to give a detailed explanation on the technique, it was remarkably similar to what I saw on the Louie Bellson/Murray Spivack video. I received a photo and letter from Frank Siegfried that does explain the technique rather well. "I am enclosing a photo of dear Billy on which he writes 'To Frank- My Star Pupil Billy Gladstone'". Apparently, Siegfried took

Siegfried's autographed photo of Billy Gladstone, Courtesy Frank Siegfried

several lessons from Gladstone. Siegfried continues "He was very generous with his praise-because I certainly was very far from being his 'Star Pupil'. He had dozens of 'Star Pupils' in his lifetime!!!-BUT- what he always did say was that I was the one individual who understood his theory and practice of letting the energy of the drumhead be the source of energy to achieve fantastic stick tech-

Gladstone with autograph to John Noonan, Author's collection

nique and speed. The trick was to control that energy on the rebound of the head. That is why the stick in the left hand had to lay 'unsqeezed' in the 'cradle' opening

between the bottom of the left hand thumb and the forefinger. This particular picture illustrates that very clearly. In other words one should play the instrument with the forefinger of the left hand-and the middle finger of the right hand-NOT-with the wrists and arms. It all gets down to the fingers. You never hit the drum-you play the head and take the fullest advantage (of the head energy) and control the rebound with your fingers". I have seen this photo several times and it does appear Billy is demonstrating his grip. The bottom left photo (same as Siegfried's) was autographed to John Noonan by Billy. Noonan was an important educational authority on snare drumming. Billy made two six by fourteen snares for Noonan in 1950, one in black lacquer, the other in natural birdseye maple. The nameplate for these drums is engraved "Specially designed for John Noonan by Billy Gladstone 1950".

Louie Bellson's Gladstone drum, Author's collection

Louie Bellson's Gladstone snare has an interesting heritage. Bellson, " I met Billy in '42 when I joined Benny's (Goodman) band on my way to New York. We played The Hotel New Yorker. When I went over to see Phil Grant he said 'You've got to meet Billy Gladstone'. Shelly Manne had told me about Billy, too. Shelly had a complete set (of Gretsch Gladstones). I don't know whatever happened to that set. I hope they've got it in some museum. It was gorgeous just to look at. Later on, in 1956, I was with the Tommy Dorsey Band at the Statler Hotel. We had about fifteen minutes before a radio broadcast and Billy Gladstone walks in with this case. He said 'This is for you'. I took that drum out of the case and Billy waited to hear the drum. Now, you've got saxophone players and trumpet players in a big band, they don't know much about drums. All during the radio program, not only Tommy (Dorsey), but all the guys in the band turned around going like this to me (thumbs up).

They all came to me afterwards and asked 'What were you playing on back there'? That's how great the drum sounded. There's a lot of history with that drum. I lent it to my brother because he was stuck for a drum. I said, 'Look, this is a prized possession'. Somebody stole it from him. It was gone for a long time. Bob Yeager, who had a drum shop in Hollywood (Professional Drum Shop) got a phone call from Johnny Miller who had a drum shop in Kansas City. He (Miller) said a guy had just brought a drum in (with Louie Bellson's name

"Specially Designed for Louie Bellson", Author's collection

on the side). Bob Yeager said 'Get it! Pay the guy. I don't care what it is and ship it out to me. It belongs to Louie'. When Yeager got the drum he put it on the shelf to exhibit it. This was right before the earthquake in '72. That was the only drum that fell off the shelf. Luckily, it didn't crack the shell, but it bent some of the hardware. We immediately sent it to Teddy Reed in Florida who took over all (some) of Billy Gladstone's material. Ted put it back in shape. I gave it to Harvey Mason

Louie Bellson, his Gladstone snare, and the author at the 1999 Hollywood Vintage and Custom Drum Show, Author's collection

because he had heard so much about the drum. Harvey has a very beautiful wife. He said 'I'll give you anything. I'll even give you my wife!' He said, 'That snare drum, Lou, is the greatest snare drum I ever played on in my life'. It's just a magnificent work of art". After I acquired the drum from Louie

Bob Yeager's method book "Chop" Builders, Author's collection

Bellson, I brought it to the 1999 *Hollywood Vintage and Custom Drum Show* where Louie was conducting a clinic. Bellson not only related the above story but treated the audience to a performance on his Gladstone drum. The drum is also pictured on the cover of Bob Yeager's *"Chop" Builders*.

In 1992 I received a letter from Frankie Phelan, a teacher/musician residing in St. Catharines, Ontario Canada. Phelan's seven by fourteen black lacquer Gladstone drum was made in 1955. Included in his letter, Phelan sent me copies of letters written to him by Billy Gladstone. I am including them as I think it is interesting to see the negotiation process for a Billy Gladstone custom snare.

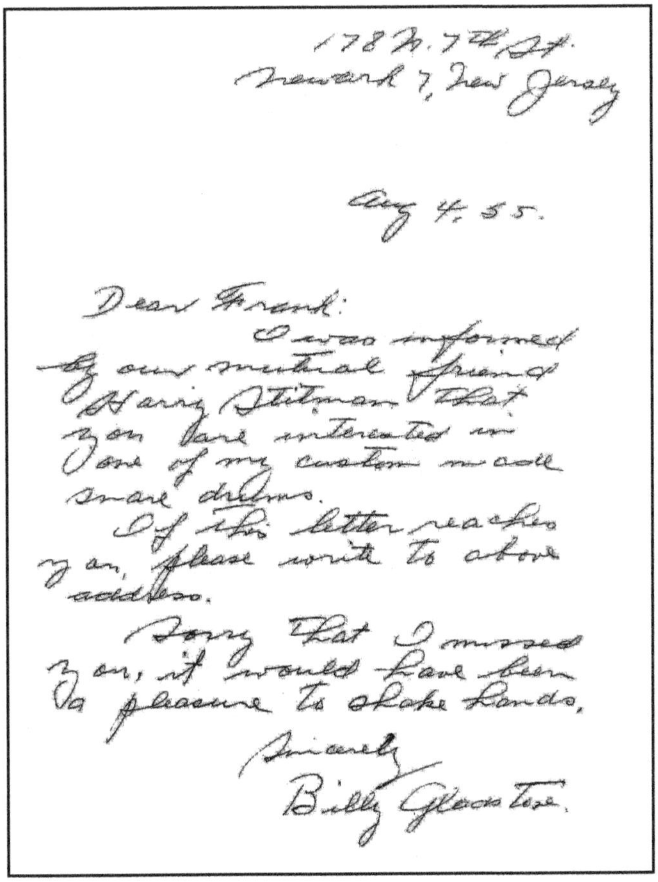

August 4, 1955 Billy Gladstone letter to Frank Phelan, Courtesy Frank Phelan

Aug. 4, 55

Dear Frank:
I was informed by our mutual friend Harry Stitman that you are interested in one of my custom made snare drums. If this letter reaches you, please write to the above address. Sorry that I missed you, it would have been a pleasure to shake hands.
Sincerely,

Billy Gladstone

Harry Stitman was the percussionist for the NBC orchestra. His seven by fourteen black lacquer Gladstone snare was made in 1950. Apparently, Billy did not have Phelan's address so he simply used only the city address.

Aug . 10, 55

Dear Frank:
I was more than surprised to receive an answer to my letter that did not have an address. You must be pretty well known in your home town.

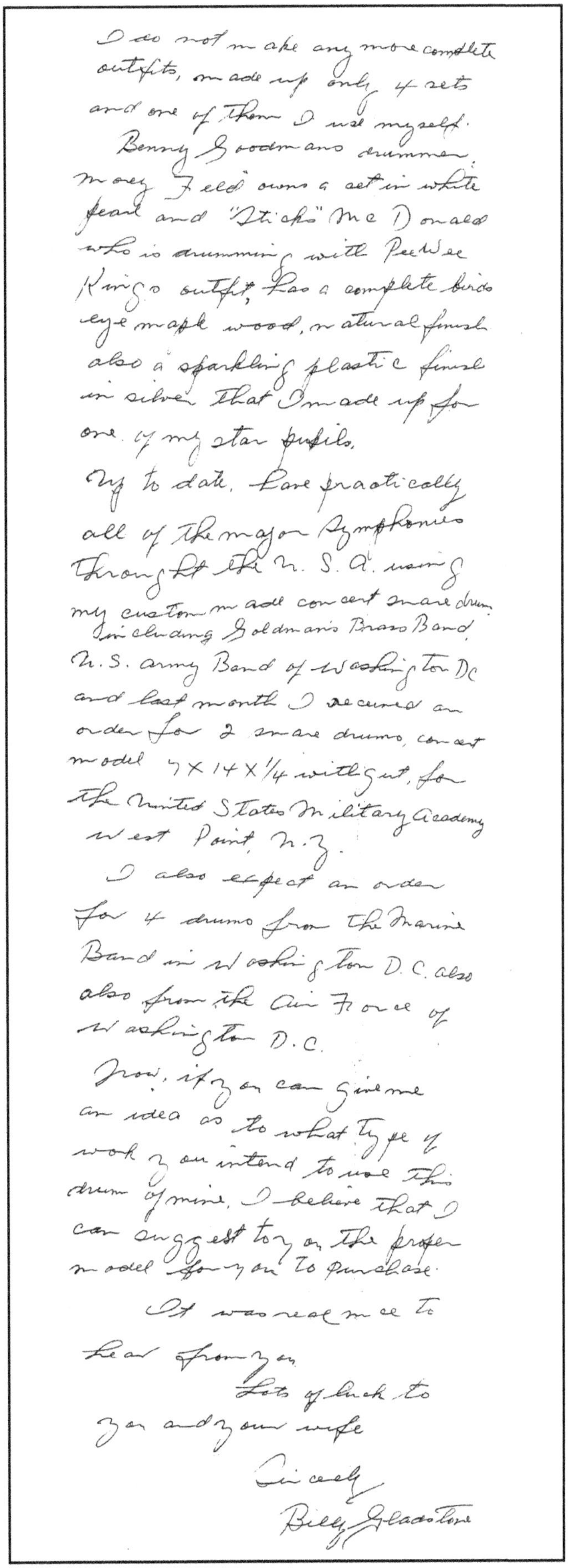

August 10, 1955 Billy Gladstone letter to Frank Phelan, Courtesy Frank Phelan

I really did forget that you once took a single lesson and that you have met my wife at the time. She was really a wonderful person and I miss her dreadfully. I do not make any more complete outfits, made up only 4 sets and one of them I use myself.

Benny Goodman's drummer "Morey Feld" owns a set in white pearl and "Sticks" Mc Donald who is drumming with Pee Wee King's outfit, has a complete birds eye maple wood natural finish, also a sparkling plastic finish in silver that I made up for one of my star pupils.

Up to date, have practically all of the major symphonies throughout the U.S.A. using my custom made concert snare drums including Goldman's Brass Band, three (3) snare drums for the U.S. Army band of Washington, DC, and last month I received an order for 2 snare drums, concert model 7 X 14 X 1/4 with gut, for the United States Military Academy West Point, N.Y.

I also expect an order for 4 drums from the Marine Band in Washington, DC also from the Air Force of Washington, DC.

Now, if you can give me an idea as to what type of work you intend to use this drum of mine, I believe that I can suggest to you the proper model for you to purchase.

It was nice to hear from you.

Lots of luck to you and your wife.

Sincerely,
Billy Gladstone

Frank had inquired as to the availability of complete Gladstone drum sets, to which Billy declined. Gladstone included a testimonial letter from the United States Army Band.

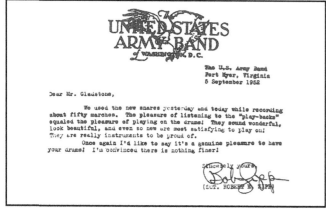

September 5, 1952 US Army Band letter to Billy Gladstone,
Courtesy Frank Phelan

The U.S. Army Band
Fort Myer, Virginia
5 September 1952

Dear Mr. Gladstone,
We used the new snares yesterday and today while recording about fifty marches. The pleasure of listening to the "play-backs" equaled the pleasure of playing the drums! They sound wonderful, look beautiful, and even so new are most satisfying to play on! They are really instruments to be proud of.

Once again, I'd like to say it has been a genuine pleasure to have your drums! I'm convinced there are none finer!

Sincerely yours,
Sgt. Robert E. Zipp

Then Phelan received the following letter from Gladstone postmarked September 17, 1955.

September 17, 1955 Billy Gladstone letter to Frank Phelan,
Courtesy Frank Phelan

Dear Frank:

Received your letter also check for (100.00) one hundred dollars ($740 in 2006 dollars), many thanks for same.

I have already started to work on your drum and will do my best to comply with your wishes.

The radio dial overtone control is one of the important features on the Billy Gladstone custom made snare drum. (Should have mentioned this first) I have already almost fully completed one of my symphonic snare drums that I had in mind to exhibit at the Columbia University College here in N.Y. however, it is going to be yours.

Today, I had the personalized name plate hand engraved with your name on it and tomorrow will try to have same chrome plated.

When fully completed, will ship snare drum to-
Mr. Frank Phelan
c/o Mrs. E. Foley
175 Herman St.
Buffalo 11, N.Y.
By railway Express.

I am now located in the heart of Radio City which makes things for me a little more comfortable.

Drop me a line as soon as possible as I am anxious to get your reaction.

Kindest regards to you and Mrs. Phelan.
Sincerely,
Billy Gladstone

Phelan had inquired about the tone control.

October 2, 1955 **Billy Gladstone letter to Frank Phelan,** Courtesy Frank Phelan

Sunday Oct. 2nd, 55
Dear Frank:

I have finally completed the snare drum and must say it is a masterpiece.

Just as soon as I will receive the remaining balance, shall waste no time in shipping the drum to you...

Sincerely,
Billy Gladstone

October 6, 1955 **Billy Gladstone letter to Frank Phelan,** Courtesy Frank Phelan

Oct. 6, 55
Dear Frank:

Shipped your snare drum today and many thanks for the money order that I also received this very day.

This is the second letter that I have written to you but somehow or other I forgot to place stamps on the envelope. Doubt very much whether you will receive that particular letter.

The express charge was only $3.78 ($27.97 in 2006 dollars) but it is on me with my compliments.

Will appreciate it very much if you will take the trouble to ship by parcel post the fiber case to-
"Carroll Drum Service"
209 West 48th St.
New York, N.Y. as I have borrowed it from there.
Please write to me as soon as you can. I am anxious to get your opinion on the masterpiece.
My best wishes and lots of luck.

Sincerely,
Billy Gladstone

While Billy was constructing the Frank Phelan drum, Gladstone was the percussionist for the Broadway musical *Plain and Fancy* at the Mark Helinger Theatre on Broadway and 51st Street in New York. In 1992 I was fortunate to procure the Beimel ("star pupil") silver sparkle Gladstone set that Billy describes in his letter to Phelan. The size

configurations (the same as the other three sets he assembled) are: six by fourteen snare, nine by thirteen tom tom, sixteen by sixteen floor tom, and fourteen by twenty two inch bass drum. The floor tom has nine lugs. I have been told that Gladstone incorporated nine lugs so the three legs would be spaced evenly between the lugs. Billy used a Premier tom tom mount, continuing his affinity for Premier hardware. Eddie Caccavale, drummer in New York City,

Saul Leslie Beimel, Author's collection

told me he met Saul Leslie Beimel (pronounced Bimel') ca 1955. Beimel was playing in a jazz group on a day cruise ship around Manhattan. Caccavale said Beimel was the only drummer he knew who could roll with one hand.

Desiring more information on Gladstone custom sets, I went in search of Harold "Sticks" McDonald, drummer for Pee Wee King. Sticks, who owned one of four Gladstone sets, was such a colorful character I decided to do a feature article of him for *Modern Drummer* ("Portraits, Sticks McDonald Country Swinger" December 1996). "I was playing with Pee Wee King (country-swing band famous for 'Slow Poke' and 'Tennessee Waltz') at the time and we were scheduled to appear on the *Kate Smith Show* and the *Milton Berle Show*. When I arrived in New York, I made an appointment with

"Star Pupil" Beimel Gladstone set, Author's collection

"Sticks" and the author, Author's collection

Billy to see if he would accept me as a student. We met at his apartment and I remember him saying, 'Play me a roll'. Well, I mustered up the best open roll I could and was pleased when Billy responded with, 'You've got nice hands'. Later he told me 'Don't let anyone play your drums because it changes the character and tone of them'. I said 'Billy that sounds almost mystical'. He said 'Well, I guess I must be mystical because I have had it happen to me. They step up and played my drum at Radio City Music Hall and it would take me twenty minutes to get it in tune again. They might just play a roll but some of the character of the person playing the drum is left behind. My method of playing the drums is the closest to "Zen" as you can get'". Sticks continued, "Billy's idea of playing was 'Let "it" do it. This is the idea of Zen...whatever "it" is, does the playing for you. In actual practice you can forget about what is happening all around you and be a part of the instrument. Forget the people in the band. You listen to them with an inner ear'". Stanley Spector is quoted with "I met Billy when he was in Boston with *My Fair Lady*. He gave me a lesson on his technique. I never met anyone who's been that helpful. Billy was a zen master with drumsticks. He knew how to go with nature".[38] (For those of you interested in this "Zen" approach to music I recommend reading Kenny Werner's *Effortless Mastery,* Published by Jamey Aebersold Jazz, Inc. ISBN 1-56224-003-X). Sticks then talked about his drums, "My set was special because it was all birdseye maple with gold plating on the snare drum. I remember Billy telling me how difficult it was to get a bass drum with that much figured wood. He told me he rejected three shells before he settled on the one for my set. Unfortunately, I loaned my set to Dave Gardner, who was working in a club in Bessemer, Alabama. Supposedly, there was quite a rivalry going on between the night clubs in Bessemer, and the

"Sticks" and Shelly Manne seated at Gladstone set, Author's collection

club where Gardner was playing got torched-burned to the ground, including my set. I pulled my hair out for a week after. I hate to think what that set would be worth today, but Billy only charged me $500 ($3700 in 2006 dollars) for the whole set in 1955! He wasn't in it for the money".[39] Sticks told me that wasn't his first Billy Gladstone drum. "I had a beautiful set of Midnight Blue pearl Gretsch drums when I was on tour with Pee Wee and asked Billy to make a snare to match in 1952. I wish I still had that drum but I sold it many years ago". Later, I found the drum and told Sticks that the owner, who lived in Nashville, would not part with the drum. Sticks asked "Does it still have my name on it"? When I con-

"Sticks" receiving his first Gladstone drum from Billy at his NY apartment, Author's collection

firmed that it did, Sticks, who once lived in Nashville, said "You know I'm still really good friends with the police chief in Nashville. How about I call him and tell him this guy stole my drum"? (Did I mention that Sticks was quite a character?) I responded "Well, Sticks, I really want the drum but not that bad. Let me work on him a while". Unfortunately, Sticks died of cancer shortly thereafter. I received a note from his bereaved wife Dottie thanking me for the *Modern Drummer* Portrait article. "It really gave him a lift when he needed it most". I then made a

Merry Christmas — and a Happy New Year

Sticks, Dottie and "Bongo" + his mark

1953

Photo of a playful "Sticks" and Dottie Christmas card, Author's collection

[38] "Billy Remembered" *Modern Drummer*, vol. 5 no. 7 Modern Drummer Publications, Inc.,Cedar Grove, NJ, 1981

[39] "Billy Gladstone Custom Drums" by Chet Falzerano, *Percussive Notes*, vol. 32 no. 4, Percussive Arts Society, Lawton, OK, 19941

concerted effort and finally acquired the "Sticks" Gladstone drum. The nameplate is engraved "Specially designed for Harold 'Sticks' McDonald WAVE Louisville, Ky. By Billy Gladstone". I called Dottie for

"Sticks",   Author's collection

an explanation. "That is where our romance began", she said. "Our first date was Sticks inviting me to the TV station (WAVE-TV) where he was playing".

I received from Eddie Jenkins, drummer for Bunny Berigan, a letter that Billy Gladstone wrote to him in 1956.

June 1956 Billy Gladstone letter to Eddie Jenkins,   Courtesy Eddie Jenkins

Dear Eddie
This may appear somewhat of a new sound but I happened to be in "Childs" restaurant on Broadway and 47th St. and it started to rain so badly that after

being here for two hours, have decided to write you a note.

I have finally connected with a musical on Broadway that is without a doubt one of the best hits in years. I am now the understudy for the drummer of this particular musical "My Fair Lady" and am to take his place while he is on vacation. After that I am to take the tour company that is being formed to go out some time late in the season.

Meanwhile I am constantly picking up on my business. The drums are selling more than ever, it has started to roll by themselves (clever eh?). Sold (3) three snare drums to the Marine Band of Washington, D.C. (2) two to the Military Academy Band of West Point N.Y. (1) one to the Chicago Symphony (1) one to Philadelphia Symp. (1) one to Juliard student and (1) one to Canada Symp. Orch. Also (1) one to Ted Reed-used to be with Milt Herth Trio, also to Sid Bulking who is Dick Haymes drummer, and above all, a birds eye maple snare drum to Louie Bellson. He was so happy with it that he wrote out a check for $300.00 ($2187 in 2006 dollars). How about that?

My drum pad is doing very nicely, so does my newly developed vibe "No-break" mallets.

It has taken me exactly one year and two months to be feeling like myself again...was a walking skeleton. Have sold the entire house including all our furniture and at present live all alone in the heart of Radio City section. Gave the "princess" away to the nurse who took care of Dottie.

Please forgive this type of letter, just happened to have this with me.

If you ever happen to visit Washington D.C. look up Robert Stewart. He is the drummer with the Marine Band, a swell guy.

Glad you like your B.G. snare.

My best to your lovely family.

Sincerely,
Billy

The drummer, for whom Gladstone was the understudy in the Broadway musical *My Fair Lady,* was Al Ross. Al Ross died in 1990, but his son Ken is keeping his father's legacy alive playing in the Stamford, CT area on his father's Gladstone drums. One is a snare that Billy made up for Al in a six by fourteen size, black lacquer and gold plating.

My Fair Lady Program, Author's collection

Al Ross also got Billy's Black Lacquer set, same sizes as the Beimel set but in gold plated hardware. The nameplate reads "Billy Gladstone with *My Fair Lady*". Both Al and Billy played these drums during the Broadway run of *My Fair Lady* but when Billy accompanied the tour company on the road, he used

Al Ross' Gladstone drum, Courtesy Ken Ross

his gold Radio City Music Hall drum. In fact, the autographed photos to Frank Siegfried and John Noonan were taken at the Schubert Theatre in

Chicago when Billy was on tour with *My Fair Lady.* Ken wrote to me, "When I was 13 years old my father brought home about

Billy Gladstone's *My Fair Lady* set, Courtesy Ken Ross

six of Billy's shells-and a bag of Billy's hardware. My father ended up giving it all to Frank Ipolitto of Frank Ipolitto's Drum shop in N.Y.C. Frank's store went out of business not long after he passed away. I wish I knew what happened to that stuff. My father died last year. I can tell you-he had the deepest respect for Billy. Arnie Lang (of Lang Percussion, more later) told me when he was walking on Canal Street (N.Y.C.) and noticed one of those junk stores selling Billy's hardware in boxes on the sidewalk. At that time he just took a few pieces. I bet he regrets that now". At one time, Al Ross also owned Gene Krupa's Gladstone drum bearing the name-plate "Gene Krupa The World's Most Renowned Drummer From Billy Gladstone".

Gene Krupa's Gladstone drum, Author's collection

Glenn Robinson, while playing at the Cincinnati Symphony, had a Gladstone drum made in 1953. "I was hearing a lot about Gladstone drums. The first time I heard one was in the early 50's when the American Ballet Theatre was touring through Cincinnati. They only toured with a small pit

orchestra and would augment it with local players. I was the principal percussionist with the Cincinnati Symphony, so I got the call. Stanley Koor was the percussionist with the tour group and he had his seven by fourteen black lacquer drum with him. I

Stanley Koor's Gladstone drum, Author's collection

was really impressed with the drum, but they were very expensive at the time...$300.00 ($2228 in 2006 dollars). I know that doesn't sound like much now, but keep in mind, a Ludwig Super Sensitive was only about $85.00 ($631 in 2006 dollars). The next time I heard a Gladstone drum was when the Boston Symphony came to Cincinnati. Harold Farberman, the principal percussionist, had a seven by fourteen birdseye maple drum that he used for the solo part on Ravel's 'Lavalse'. Usually this solo gets drowned out by the orchestra but not this time. You could hear every note with his drum. I went to see Farberman after the program and he said 'I would recommend Gladstone's drums to anyone'. That was enough for me so I got Gladstone's address from Harold and wrote to Billy. At the time, in the early 50's, Gladstone wouldn't sell you a drum unless you were with a major symphony. Later, he made drums for anyone who would order one, but in the beginning of his drum making career he wanted to be represented by all the major symphonies. Billy was a real gentleman, but he was also eccentric. You had to do everything his way. I remember when we were negotiating for the drum I asked Billy 'What if I don't like the drum'? His response was 'Glenn, you sound like the kind of person I don't want to sell a drum to'. That was it...end of story. A few months later, the symphony was on tour and we were scheduled to play at Carnegie Hall. I called Billy and told him I was going to be in New York and could we meet. We set up a meeting at his apartment, which was small but well furnished. He was working on a seven by fourteen birdseye drum with gut snares. After we talked for a while he said 'I'll finish this one up for you' which he did and sent it to me in '53. I played that drum in the Cincinnati Symphony for the next nine years, but in 1962 it was stolen. I never leave instruments in the car, but my wife Marinka and I were forced to leave the drum in our locked car. When I came back, the window was broken and the drum was gone. I reported it to the police, but nothing came of it.

I got the Krupa Gladstone drum through my wife. She had left the Cincinnati Symphony for a local Broadway theatre group. She became good friends with Al Ross who was the percussionist traveling with the tour group of *Hello Dolly, Camelot, Fiddler on the Roof, King and I*, etc. We had him over for dinner several times. One night in '65 he shows up with the Krupa drum in the trunk of his car. He knew my drum was stolen so he proposed a trade. At the time, plastic heads were taking over the market and good calf timpani heads were becoming hard to get. He offered to trade the drum for four heads. That was it...four heads! I'm sure it was also

because we were good friends, but I was sure happy to get the drum. Gene and I were acquainted, so I tried to contact him about the drum, but unfortunately he died before we could connect. That drum and I have been around the world several times together...Europe, the Orient, everywhere. It saw a lot of use. Later, when I was with the Kansas City Philharmonic, I remember Vince Bilardo, principal percussionist, tried the drum. He looked over to the other percussionists and said 'Listen to the balls on this drum'. I had to laugh". It should be noted, Krupa, as a Slingerland endorser, was very loyal. He was with Slingerland throughout his career. Many of his colleagues changed brands almost as often as they changed socks. For Krupa to stray from the nest and acquire another snare, even a custom one, was indeed laudatory. A photo of Gene playing the drum appears in Milt Hinton's book *Bass Line* (Temple University Press, ISBN 0-87722-681-4). It pictures Gene playing his Gladstone drum in a recording session with Thelma Carpenter in 1963.

Glenn Robinson also assisted one of his colleagues at the Cincinnati Symphony in acquiring a drum in 1959. Trudy Drummond Muegel: "I wanted one of Billy's drums, so I arranged a meeting with him at his hotel

Gene Krupa playing his Gladstone drum at a Thelma Carpenter session in 1963. Courtesy Milt Hinton

room. He was on tour with *My Fair Lady.* I went with Glenn Robinson, one of my associates. He knew Billy and already had a Gladstone drum. I chose a black lacquer seven inch drum. Billy said he would send me the drum after he had the nameplate engraved with my name, but I insisted that I get the drum right then and there. The nameplate on the drum was already engraved 'Billy Gladstone Radio City Music Hall'. Unfortunately, Billy died before he could have a nameplate engraved for me.

Still waiting, Author's collection

Trudy Drummond Muegel's Gladstone drum, Courtesy Trudy Drummond Muegel

I don't really mind though; it's an honor to have Billy's name on my drum"[40]. Stanley Koor's desire also won out over his patience. When Koor's drum was made in 1951, "I was auditioning for major symphonies after graduating from Juliard. I told Billy I wanted my drum to include the symphony. Billy said 'When you get the job I'll have the nameplate engraved'". Koor continued, "I never got a symphony job so I left the nameplate blank". Before he sold his drums, Billy's samples either had a blank nameplate or a Billy Gladstone Radio City Music Hall nameplate.

Gladstone's "No Break" mallets come with an interesting story. In 1996 I acquired a promotional photo taken in 1956 for the movie *The Benny Goodman Story.* It was taken during the *Steve Allan Show* to promote the movie which featured Steve Allan as Benny Goodman. Harry Sheppard, pictured on vibes, recalls "We were playing 'Moonglow' when that picture was taken. I remember it like it was yesterday". "Harry Sheppard was instrumental in the development of Gladstone's 'No Break' vibe mallets. Sheppard first met Gladstone in 1956. Sheppard was playing with Sol Yaged's group at the Metropole in New York City. Yaged played clarinet, Sheppard played vibes, Kenny Kersey was on piano, Mort Herbert played bass and Cozy Cole was on drums. Of their first meeting Sheppard says: 'Billy came in to see his friend Cozy Cole, and Cozy introduced me to him. The first thing Gladstone said to me was, "I've never seen anybody but Lionel Hampton play as hard as you do". You see, the owner of the Metropole, Ben Harriman, insisted that the bands play full volume- no ballads. The music critics used to say, "It's like the jazz is shot out of a cannon when you walk into the place". The doors of the club were never closed during business hours. Harriman wanted

The Benny Goodman Story promotional photo with Skitch Henderson, Steve Allen and Sol Yaged with Harry Sheppard on vibes using the Gladstone "No Break" mallets, Author's collection

[40] IBID

everyone in Times Square to hear the music. When Sol Yaged said he wanted to add me to his group, Harriman insisted that I audition because he didn't think vibes could maintain the volume level he required. Harriman was hard of hearing and wore a hearing aid. For my audition Harriman walked across the street to Howard's Clothes, stood in the doorway and turned his hearing aid off! He signaled me to start playing. After a few minutes, he appeared in the doorway of the Metropole and gave Sol the nod. I passed the audition and got the gig. We played so loud I actually broke vibe bars in half-at least one every six months. You can imagine what I did to rattan-handle mallets. If they didn't break, they simply bent out of shape in no time'. Gladstone was impressed with Sheppard's playing. Sheppard remembers Gladstone's words, 'It's very exciting, but you must go through a lot of mallets. I'd like you to help me develop a mallet that won't bend or break'. Sheppard agreed; however, he didn't think much more about it. A few weeks later, Gladstone came to the Metropole with some prototype mallets. Gladstone designed the heads of the mallets out of wood in the shape of a wheel. He then had rubber bands of varying thickness and density that wrapped around the wheel like a tire. The variations in the rubber resulted in a hard or soft sound. In addition, he tried all kinds of plastic shafts, as described in his patent filed in 1954, but eventually they all failed. Gladstone would come into the Metropole with a package of two or three dozen mallets. The stage at the Metropole was above the bar and Gladstone would toss the package on stage to Sheppard. Gladstone even had the mallets numbered, and as they failed, he would check the number off the list. Sheppard said this process went on for some time until Gladstone tried fiberglass shafts, which worked perfectly. Sheppard commented 'As hard as I played, I never broke a shaft. The heads would some-

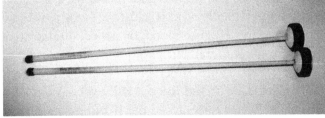

Gladstone "No Break" Mallets, Author's collection

times fly off, but the shafts would never break. Billy was really pleased. I thought they were fantastic, not only because they wouldn't break, but I thought they were much more accurate. Playing as hard as I did, I found that

rattan shafts were too flexible. They would whip at high volume and sometimes strike between the bars. Gladstone's fiberglass shafts were rigid enough that this distortion didn't occur. Some of the guys didn't like them because they weren't flexible, but for my needs they were perfect. Without a doubt, Billy Gladstone started the trend for fiberglass mallets that continues to this day', Sheppard says. 'A lot of manufacturers offer fiberglass mallets, but when Gladstone developed his "No Break" mallets, everyone else was using rattan. I don't think manufacturers (then) particularly liked using fiberglass because they last too long. You know, planned obsolescence'".[41]

Joe Morello, "After that one lesson I had with Gladstone in New York, I went out to the West Coast when I joined Brubeck. I was with him for twelve or thirteen years doing a lot of one nighters on the road. Every two months we'd take a week or two off for a rest, back in San Francisco. I noticed that Billy was playing with *My Fair Lady*, so I went to the (War Memorial Opera House) to see him and we got together. Billy smuggled me into the orchestra pit and I'd sit right next to him. I watched him for maybe two weeks straight. Later, we went up to my apartment and have coffee with brandy. The way I got him to teach me was while we were talking I started hitting a practice pad all wrong...just putting him on. He said 'Oh no, you know better than that. I guess you really want me to teach you'. I said 'Yeah, I'll pay you anything you want'. He finally gave me lessons but he wouldn't take a cent for it. Every night we would work together. He was

My Fair Lady at the War Memorial Opera House, San Francisco, Author's collection

41 "Billy Gladstone 'No Break' Vibe Mallets" by Chet Falzerano, *Percussive Notes,* vol. 35 no. 1, Percussive Arts Society, Lawton, OK, 1997

very pleased with what I did, I guess. It was an incredible thing that put the finishing touch on my technique. He was a very kind, gentle man...very technical, very particular. He had a very unique way of playing...a nice touch. He got a beautiful sound out of the drum. He never squeezed the drumstick. It was always very loose and free. You could hear the 'ring' of the (drumstick) wood when he played". I asked Joe to elaborate, "If you clench two sticks in you hands and hit them together you hear a stiff 'thump' sound. If you hold the sticks loose, you'll hear the ring of the wood. That's important especially when playing a cymbal. You get a true sound. When you hold the stick tight, you choke everything. He was a tremendous technician. There's no question about it. He later gave me a (voice) recording, saying I was one of the first guys that really understood the technique he was using. It was so nice. One funny story when we were hanging out in San Francisco, he was looking for a wood block. We went to (Kenny William's) Drumland where they had a big box with maybe thirty or forty wood blocks inside. One by one he went through them...*Tick*, 'No', *Tick*, 'No, that's not it'...*Tick*, 'No, No'...*Tick*, 'No'...*Tick, Tick*, 'No'. I was thinking it was just a silly wood block...what the hell are we listening to? Finally, *Tick*, 'There it is'. He was so into sound; it was incredible. A very soft spoken gentleman. He never talked about his own ability. I never asked him who he studied with. I guess I forgot". I said I have been researching the man for over twenty years and never found out who Gladstone's mentors were. Morello said "Maybe his name was 'Lamont Kranston' or maybe it was *The Shadow* or something (laughs)".

Billy Gladstone continued building his drums throughout the late fifties while traveling with the tour company of *My Fair Lady.* Ted Reed, "I found out that drummers in the various cities where the show played had gone to see the show, but couldn't take their eyes off Billy. They had to go a second time to see the show".[42] One of the last Gladstone custom-built drums was for Herb Brochstein, founder of Pro Mark. The drum, made in 1961, was a six by fourteen birdseye maple. I received a letter from Brochstein with a copy of an endorsement letter he received from Billy written on *My Fair Lady* stationary.

Gladstone endorses Pro Mark, Courtesy Herb Brochstein

Brockstein's
2211 Chenvert St.
Houston, Texas

Dear Herb,

"P R O - M A R K"
Snare Drum Sticks that I am
now using, are without a doubt
"THE FINEST EVER"

Most Sincerely,
Billy Gladstone

Brochstein explains, "I ran across this letter from Billy which he had framed and sent to me before we ever met personally. He (Gladstone) really did like the Pro-Mark 2B oak wood tip stick". Gladstone also sent an autographed photo with the inscription "To-My Pal 'Herb Brochstein' With Admiration, Billy Gladstone". Ted Reed, "Billy was also a very fine pianist. He once asked me if I knew he played piano. When I told him I didn't, he rented a studio at Nola's on Broadway and taped his version of 'The Minute Waltz'. I still have that tape and it's an absolutely perfect performance of the piece". Reed sent me a copy of the tape early on in our relation-

---

42 "A Tribute to Billy Gladstone" by Ted Reed, *Modern Drummer*, vol. 5 no. 7, Modern Drummer Publications, Inc., Cedar Grove, NJ, 1981

ship. I, in turn, later sent him a copy of a tape that I unearthed of Gladstone playing a xylophone medley of "Ida" and "Some of These Days" recorded on the *Major Bowes Capitol Theatre* (Radio) *Program*. Ted was most appreciative and commented, "Billy did a good job on the 'woodpile'. I heard him play many, many times-he was a great musician". Few recordings remain of Gladstone's performances. The only other substantial example I found is a *Radio City Music Hall Souvenir Album*. Gladstone is not identified on the jacket, however Erno Rapee is, and Billy was

Radio City Music Hall Souvenir Album **under the direction of Erno Rapee,**
Author's collection

the percussionist under Rapee's direction at the Music Hall. Reed continues, "I also clearly recall the last year of Billy's life. He was in New York on a break from *My Fair Lady* road show and decided to have a much needed hernia operation. Cancer was discovered. Billy continued with the show but was failing fast by the time they reached Boston in August of '61. Finally, the orchestra leader convinced Billy to return to New York for a rest. I knew he was in serious trouble the day he walked into my studio. He was brown as a coffee bean. Billy was in and out of Flower of Fifth Avenue Hospital in New York several times before he finally died in October. He had requested his ashes be spread around the Statue of Liberty. I don't know if that request was ever carried out, but I

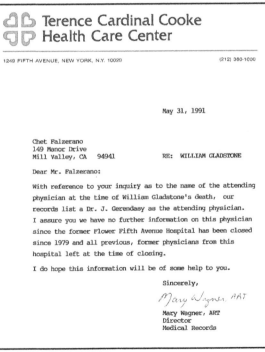

Terence Cardinal Cooke Health Care Center, formerly Flower of Fifth Avenue Hospital, Author's collection

do know that the legend lives on. Billy Gladstone was one of the greatest drummers of all time and a beautiful person with a heart as big as New York City itself. I'm very proud to be able to say I knew him, and that he was my friend".[43]

I wrote to the Flower of Fifth Avenue Hospital, now the Terence Cardinal Cooke Health Care Center for information about Billy's final stay there. Mary Wagner, Director of Medical Records responded, "With reference to your inquiry as to the name of the attending physician at the time of Billy Gladstone's death, our records list a Dr. J. Gerendasy as the attending physician. I assure you we have no further information on this physician since the former Flower of Fifth Avenue Hospital has been closed since 1979 and all previous, former physicians from this hospital left at the time of closing". Gladstone's obituary in the October 6, 1961 *New York Times*, in part, reads "Billy Gladstone, a Band Drummer-Musician, 68, Dies-Devised Orchestral Equipment". Listing Billy's many achievements, both musical and as an inventor, it singles out, "The Gladstone drum, more costly than a machine-made drum, has been used by Gene Krupa, Buddy Rich, Sticks MacDonald [sic], and other top-flight drummers".

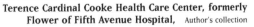

---

43 Ibid

Fortunately for us, Billy Gladstone's legacy does live on in several ways. Gladstone was inducted into the Percussive Arts Society Hall of Fame in 1978. He has been the subject of many articles and various artists have written about and demonstrated their interpretation of the Gladstone finger technique. Foremost among these artists is Morris "Arnie" Lang. Along with his forty plus years performing with the world renowned New York Philharmonic Orchestra, his thirty plus years as Professor/Head of Percussion Department/Head of Graduate Program at the Conservatory of Music, Brooklyn College, Lang is also President of Lang Percussion, manufacturing timpani and Lang/Gladstone snare drums.

PAS Hall of Fame, Courtesy Morris Lang

Lang met Billy Gladstone while he was a student at Juliard. "My classmates at Juliard were the likes of Harold Farberman, Buster Bailey, Mickey Bookspan, Arthur Press, and my teachers were Saul Goodman and Moe Goldenberg...it was intense. It was Harold Farberman, about two years my senior, who was the first of the student group to get a legit gig. I'll never forget him coming up to us and saying 'Hey guys, I got a job'! We were all pretty impressed when he told us it was at Radio City Music Hall. He

Morris "Arnie" Lang, Courtesy Morris Lang

asked me if I wanted to go see the show. Since I have never been to the Music Hall I was delighted. The Music Hall was going through quite a change of format (Page Purge), cutting out the bass drummer/cymbal player and adding a drumset, which was Harold's position. There was still a timpanist and snare drummer, but as the snare drummer, it turned out to be Billy's last group of shows. During one of the breaks between shows we all went downstairs to the employee lounge where there was an adjoining practice room. That's when I met Billy; Harold introduced me to him. Billy asked 'You want to play a little bit'? So we all started exercising on practice pads. Billy came over to me and pointed at my right

hand saying 'You get pain in this area, right around here, right'? I was taken by surprise, because it was true. 'You also experience pain in this part of your left wrist', pointing to the exact spot that I was having trouble. I said, 'Yeah, do you give lessons'? and within a short time I was taking my first lesson in his apartment on 54th Street and 6th Avenue. We never worked off of sheet music during any of my lessons. I was, after all, studying with Saul Goodman and Moe Goldenberg, so I did not need coaching in theory. No, our work was strictly conceptual...proper grip, natural hand positioning, controlling rebounds, relaxed approach, producing tones, that kind of thing. I was so happy to lose the tension and therefore the pain in my hands. Billy was a nice addition, coaching wise, to Goodman and Goldberg. After a time, we became more personal. Though he was starting up his drum business, his professional music life was pretty much at a standstill. Being released from the Music Hall took him by surprise. His wife was still a Rockette so they were OK financially, but you could tell it was hard on him. He told me, 'I'm not doing much of anything'. Well, I was maybe only twenty years old and actively playing club dates, weddings, bar mitzvahs, etc., so I naively offered to help him find work. Billy politely turned me down saying that wasn't what he was looking for. I remember him being very excited about a recording session he was offered

A "younger"Arnie with his Gladstone drum, Courtesy Morris Lang

shortly thereafter. It was working with a trombone concerto, a military kind of thing. He was using a snare, bass drum and a hi hat. Looking for more of a military sound from the cymbals, he wasn't happy with the results of the hi hat. He removed the footboard of the hi hat and replaced it with a canvas strap for more sensitivity and it worked well. He was constantly inventing. He made my (Gladstone custom) drum shortly after I started taking lessons in 1951. My fellow students couldn't believe I paid $175.00 ($1335 in 2006 dollars) for a snare drum. They all asked. 'What did you get that for'? Keep in mind, the top Ludwig Super Sensitive snare drum was only about $45 ($343 in 2006 dollars) in those days. I just had to have the best when I got my first gig at the Civic Center Ballet (now known as the New York Civic Center Ballet). Around the time Gladstone's wife died (in 1954) he told me he was moving to New Jersey to a house that his wife's mother had left them. I remember he was working for an organ repair shop, repairing percussion instruments in old theatre organs. He was also

Birth of a legacy, Arnie's Gladstone drum, Courtesy Morris Lang

selling off a lot of his percussion stuff. It was sad. We lost touch with each other, him moving to New Jersey and me struggling with my career.

In 1955, I got the job as assistant timpanist with the New York Philharmonic. These days, all first chair symphonic musicians have an assistant but it was a new thing back then. Saul Goodman helped me get the job. In fact, I didn't even audition. I had to play something else and the cymbal chair was open so I also got that job, not knowing a thing about symphonic cymbals. I mean, I had no symphonic cymbal experience, so I drove to the Zildjian Factory in Massachusetts with a list that Goodman gave me. Since then I have built up quite a collection". It should be noted, the "collection" has become world class, unmatched by any other symphony. The insurance alone for these cymbals is staggering. Lang continues, "I occasionally used the Gladstone snare when Buster Bailey needed a second snare for a Bolero or a Shostakovich piece. Buster actually stopped using his Gladstone because when plastic heads took over, they kept splitting due to the sharp corners of the Gladstone snare

beds. He later had the corners rounded and it worked fine, but for the longest time it sat on his mantle at home."

I then asked how Lang Percussion got started. "I was always a tinkerer, but the company started when I saw a need for traditional xylophone mallets. Most of the big manufacturers had stopped making rattan handled mallets, opting for plastic (thanks to Billy Gladstone). I had students coming in with these terrible plastic mallets that were top heavy. I was also running out of my supply of good rattan mallets. One day, as I was looking through the yellow pages for another reason, I came across this cane and rattan company in New Jersey. I took a drive over and asked, 'Can I get 3/8 inch rattan shafts'? They said, 'Sure how many one hundred pound lots do you need'? Well, I carted home two one-hundred pound bails of rattan, but found there was a lot of waste. Rattan xylophone handles need to be clear and rattan naturally grows wild with a lot of knots, so actually, the two hundred pounds yielded the correct amount. Amongst all the hardware stores on Canal Street in New York, I found the correct plastic balls for the heads, so Lang Percussion was born. I started selling to students and friends, but then moved on to dealers. Later, I got

Lang Percussion brochure, Courtesy Morris Lang

interested in castanets, importing them from Spain and then building machine castanets. (For those of you unfamiliar with this instrument, it is generally a pair of castanets mounted on a board and played by striking them by hand. See page 79 of Anthony Cirone's *The Logic Of It All*, Cirone Publications.) I quickly moved on to other projects, as I have never been interested in the business end...I liked the creative side. I got involved

The four drum set-up used in the New York Philharmonic,
Courtesy Morris Lang

with music publishing since everyone was telling me my compositions were too good and too long, wanting me to split them up into volumes. I got a table top printer (this was before home computers) and published out of the attic of my house. Then, Saul Goodman retired and asked me if I would be interested in taking over his timpani manufacturing business. I was a bit reluctant since Goodman tympani had such a bad reputation. He owned the timpani market after World War II, since all the German factories were destroyed and Ludwig and Leedy timps were not up to symphonic standards. The problem was, he (Goodman) continued with old castings of German timpani hardware made in the 20's and 30's and did not upgrade. I agreed, under the premise that I would have complete autonomy. He was happy to get the royalties and agreed. After one and a half years of trial and error I upgraded all the hardware, bowels, everything. I remember working with Goodman's machinist. He was very frustrated because Goodman's attitude was 'It's good enough'. This guy was a perfectionist, so my corrections were a godsend to him. He enjoyed the upgrade. I then asked him if he could make parts for a snare drum. He said, 'Snare drum, kettle drum...doesn't matter to me. I make parts'. I brought in a lug and the key from my Gladstone drum and he replicated them, but at a cost of $600.00. It just didn't add up finan-

cially...not if I wanted to make a profit building drums, that is. So I started making the parts myself (self-taught machinist), found a shell manufacturer, painter, etc. and the Lang Gladstone snare drum was born. To raise capital I dreamed up a subscription plan where fifty people would advance me $250 each as a down payment toward a limited edition (50 drums) $500 Gladstone drum. I was surprised, but all fifty subscriptions sold quickly. I proposed a money-back guarantee but with no time limit. I remember one of the subscribers wrote me, 'Will I get the drum before I die'? My response was 'How old did you say you were'? Don't laugh; I actually had a woman call me asking for her money back, as her husband had died! I only had one other cancellation. One of my subscribers called me to tell me he found a (vintage Ludwig) Black Beauty and needed the money. He later came back and bought a drum, though. One of the first drums I made was for the Israel Phil-

Early Lang Percussion advertisement,
Courtesy Morris Lang

harmonic and they are still using it daily. They brought it in for a tune up recently and it sounded great. When I started, the biggest difficulty I had was replicating the shells. I found a manufacturer that was able to build a 3-ply shell that Gladstone preferred, but the quality just wasn't there. I decided on Keller 8-ply shells. I have since found a manufacturer that can make an exact copy of the old Gretsch 3-ply shells, but now, most drummers are interested in the exotic wood, solid shell, stave construction kind of thing".

To supplement my Gretsch Gladstone, Billy Gladstone collection, I chose a four by fourteen Craviatto solid shell Lang Gladstone snare and a five and a half by fourteen hand hammered (by D. Picking) engraved (by John Aldridge) copper shell Lang Gladstone. I can tell you both drums are incredible. Not only do they continue the Gladstone legacy but, in fact, go beyond.

The following table lists the **Billy Gladstone Custom Drums** that I have, to date, unearthed information.

Original Owner	Date	Size	Finish/Plating	Notes	Current Status
Buster Bailey	1949	7x14	Black Lacquer/ Chrome	NY Philharmonic Nameplate engraved "Elden C. Bailey Philharmonic Orchestra New York October 1949 Drum #0"	Private collection
Mark Barnet	?	7X14	Black Lacquer/Gold	Vegas drummer	Private collection
Louie Bellson	1956	6X14	Birdseye Maple/ Chrome	Nameplate engraved "Specially Designed For Louie Bellson By Billy Gladstone 1956"	Author's collection
Saul Leslie Beimel	?	6X14/ Set	Silver Sparkle Pearl/ Chrome	One of 4 sets. Billy's "star" pupil per letter from Billy to Frank Phelan. Nameplate engraved "S.L. Beimel"	Author's collection
Kenny Bennett	?	6X14	Black Diamond Pearl/ Chrome	Blank nameplate	Private collection
Mickie Bookspan	1953	7X14	Black Lacquer/ Chrome	Philadelphia Orchestra	Private collection
Herb Brockstein	1961	6X14	Birdseye Maple/ Chrome	President Pro Mark	Private collection
Donald Bush	1953	7X14	Black Lacquer/ Chrome	Boston Pops, Pittsburg Symphony	Private collection
Sid Bulkin	?	6X14	White Pearl/Chrome	Dick Hames Orchestra, Terry Gibbs, Billy Exstine	Whereabouts unknown
Cozy Cole	Pre 1954	6X14	White Pearl/Chrome	Nameplate engraved "Cozy Cole"	Private collection
Charles Cordes	1951	6X14	Gold Lacquer/Gold	Billy's Mechanic. Nameplate engraved "To Charles Cordes Who's Expert Mechanical Ability And Kind Cooperation Made This Drum Possible December 25, 1951 Billy Gladstone"	Private collection
Trudy Drummond Muegel	1959	7X14	Black Lacquer/ Chrome	Cincinnati Symphony. "Billy died before he could have a nameplate engraved for me". Nameplate engraved "Billy Gladstone Radio City Music Hall"	Private collection
Harold Farberman	Pre 1954	7X14	Birdseye Maple/ Chrome	Followed Billy at Radio City Music Hall, Boston Symphony Orchestra, conductor.	Private collection
Morry Feld	Pre 1954	6X14/ Set	White Pearl/Chrome	One of 4 sets. Benny Goodman	Private collection
George Gabor	1954	6X14	Black Lacquer/ Chrome	NBC Orchestra, Indiana University	Whereabouts unknown
Billy Gladstone	?	7X14	Gold Lacquer/Gold	"The" drum Billy used	Private collection
Billy Gladstone	1952	6X14/ Set	Black Lacquer/ Chrome	One of 4 sets. Nameplate engraved "Billy Gladstone My Fair Lady". Billy's set he later gave to Al Ross	Private collection
Arnold Goldberg	1953	6X14	Birdseye Maple/ Chrome	New York City Ballet	Private collection

Original Owner	Date	Size	Finish/Plating	Notes	Current Status
Morris Goldenberg	?	8X14	Metal/Engraved	New York Philharmonic	Whereabouts unknown
Marty Grupp	1951	7X14	Black Lacquer/Gold	NY session drummer Kate Smith TV Show	Whereabouts unknown
Marvin Greengold	?	7X14	Birdseye Maple/ Chrome	Missing nameplate	Whereabouts unknown
Dave Gusikof	Pre 1954	6X14	Gold Lacquer/Gold	South Pacific Musical	Whereabouts unknown
Roy Harte	?	6X14	Birdseye Maple/Gold	Owner Drum City LA. Nameplate engraved "Billy Gladstone Radio City Music Hall"	Private collection
Eddie Jenkins	1956	6X14	White Pearl/Chrome	Bunny Berigan Orchestra. Stolen at gig, later recovered but missing nameplate	Private collection
Stanley Koor	1951	7X14	Black Lacquer/ Chrome	Am. Ballet Theatre, Royal Ballet. Recorded on "Caddide" & "3 Penny Opera" Nameplate blank	Author's collection
Gene Krupa	?	7X14	Black Lacquer/ Chrome	Nameplare engraved "To Gene Krupa The World's Most Renown Drummer From Billy Gladstone"	Author's collection
Arnold Lang	1951	7X14	Black Lacquer/ Chrome	NY Philharmonic, Lang Percussion. Nameplate engraved "Arnold Lang Jan 1st. 1951	Private collection
Shelly Manne	1950	6X14	Black Lacquer/Gold	Nameplate engraved "To Shelly Manne With Admiration Billy Gladstone April 9, 1950 Drum No. 1"	Private collection
Harold McDonald	1952	6X14	Midnight Blue Pearl/ Chrome	Pee Wee King. Nameplate engraved "Specially Designed For Harold 'Sticks' McDonald WAVE Louisville, Ky. By Billy Gladstone '52"	Author's collection
Harold McDonald	1955	6X14/ Set	Birdseye Maple/Gold	One of 4 sets. Loaned to Dave Gardner, burned in a club fire in Bessemer, AL	Destroyed
John Noonan	1950	6X14	Black Lacquer/ Chrome	Teacher Champaign IL. Parted out, used as prototype for Lang replicas	Destroyed
John Noonan	1950	6X14	Birdseye Maple/ Gold	Nameplate engraved "Specially designed for John Noonan by Billy Gladstone"	Private collection
Leslie Parks	Pre 1954	?	?	Fred Warring Show on Tour	Whereabouts unknown

Original Owner	Date	Size	Finish/Plating	Notes	Current Status
Wayne Pascuzzi	Pre 1954	7X14	Black Lacquer/ Chrome	Pittsburgh Symphony	Private collection
Frank Phelan	1955	7X14	Black Lacquer/ Chrome	Teacher/casual drummer Canada	Private collection
Albert Pollick	Pre 1954	?	?	New Orleans Symphony	Whereabouts unknown
Arthur C. Press	1953	7X14	Black Lacquer/ Chrome	Radio City Music Hall, Boston Symphony Orchestra. Nameplate engraved "Arthur C. Press"	Author's collection
Ted Reed	1955	6X14	Birdseye Maple/ Chrome	Author/teacher	Private collection
Ray Reilly	1958	7X14	White Pearl/Chrome	Toronto Symphony. Nameplate Engraved "Ray Reilly January 1, 1958"	Private collection
Renzo Renzi	?	6X14	Birdseye Maple/ Chrome	Chicago Symphony	Private collection
Renzo Renzi	?	7X14	Black Lacquer/ Chrome	Chicago Symphony	Private collection
Buddy Rich	?	?	?	Per NY Times obituary and MD article "Tribute to Billy Gladstone"	Whereabouts unknown
Glenn Robinson	1952	7X14	Birdseye Maple/ Chrome	Cincinnati Symphony, Stolen	Whereabouts unknown
Al Ross	1952	6X14	Black Lacquer/Gold	Broadway pit drummer	Private collection
Joe Sinai	Pre 1954	7X14/	Birdseye Maple/ Chrome	San Francisco Symphony. Nameplate engraved "To my pal Joe Sinai"	Private collection
Samual Skinner	1953	6X14/	Birdseye Maple/Gold	New York lawyer Civic Symphony of Jamestown NY	Private collection
Viola Smith	Pre 1954	6X14	Birdseye Maple/ Chrome	Phil Spitalny Orchestra	Private collection
Harry Stitman	1950	7X14	Black Lacquer/ Chrome	NBC Orchestra	Private collection
US Army Band #1	1951	7X14	Black Lacquer/ Chrome	Per Vincent Battista with Army Band in 1951	Whereabouts unknown
US Army Band #2	1951	7X14	Black Lacquer/ Chrome	Per Vincent Battista with Army Band in 1951	Whereabouts unknown

Original Owner	Date	Size	Finish/Plating	Notes	Current Status
US Army Band #3	1951	7X14	Black Lacquer/ Chrome	Per Vincent Battista with Army Band in 1951	Whereabouts unknown
US Marine Band #1	1956	7X14	Black Lacquer/ Chrome	Per Bob Stuart with Marine Band in 1956	Whereabouts unknown
US Marine Band #2	1956	7X14	Black Lacquer/ Chrome	Per Bob Stuart with Marine Band in 1956	Whereabouts unknown
US Marine Band #3	1956	7X14	White Lacquer/ Chrome	Per Bob Stuart with Marine Band in 1956	Private collection
USMA Band #1	?	6X14	White Lacquer/ Chrome	Per SFC Gallic, West Point	Private collection
USMA Band #2	?	6X14	White Lacquer/ Chrome	Per SFC Gallic, West Point	Private collection
USMA Band #3	?	6X14	White Lacquer/ Chrome	Per SFC Gallic, West Point	Private collection
Hal Wasson	1953	7X14	Black Lacquer/ Chrome	Corpus Christie Texas Symphony	Private collection
Edward B. Wuebold Jr	1958	7X14	Black Lacquer/ Chrome	Cincinnati Symphony	Private collection

- *"Pre 1954" indicates specific knowledge of when the drum was built is not known by the author, however the drum is listed in a letter dated 1954 from Billy Gladstone to George Way.*

- *59 drums built between 1949 and 1961.*

- *29 drums in the 7X14 size, 27 6X14 (4 with complete sets) 1 8X14, 3 unknown size.*

- *27 drums in black lacquer, 4 in white lacquer, 3 in gold lacquer, 14 birdseye maple, 7 pearl covered, 1 engraved drum, 3 unknown finish*

- *42 drums in private collections, 15 whereabouts unknown, 2 destroyed (one with complete set)*

Billy Gladstone's seven by fourteen
Gretsch-Gladstone with
Gladstone-type stand
Gold lacquer/Gold plating
Wire snares
Author's collection

Nick Fatool's seven by fourteen
Gretsch-Gladstone
White Oriental pearl/Gold plating
Wire snares
Author's collection
Photo by Nick Falzerano

Arthur Press' seven by fourteen
Billy Gladstone
Black lacquer/Chrome plating
Wire/Gut snares
Author's collection

Gretsch-Gladstones with Drummers'
Wheeled Console
White Oriental pearl/Chrome plating
Six and one-half by fourteen snare
with wire snares
Nine by thirteen, ten by fourteen,
and sixteen by sixteen single tension
tomtoms
Fourteen by twenty six single ten-
sion six bass drum
Courtesy Roger Turner

Shelly Manne's six by fourteen
Billy Gladstone,
Black lacquer/Gold plating
Wire snares
Courtesy of Larry Bunker

Louie Bellson's six by fourteen
Billy Gladstone
Clear lacquer Birdseye Maple/
Chrome plating
Wire snares
Author's collection

Saul Leslie "Star Pupil" Beimel's
Billy Gladstone Set
Silver Sparkle pearl/Chrome plating
Six by fourteen snare with wire snares
Nine by fourteen and sixteen by
sixteen tom toms
Fourteen by twenty two bass drum
Author's collection
Photo by Nick Falzerano

Saul Beimel's six by fourteen
Billy Gladstone
Silver Sparkle pearl/Chrome plating
Wire snares
Author's collection

Gene Krupa's seven by fourteen
Billy Gladstone
Black lacquer/Chrome plating
Gut snares
Author's collection

Harold "Sticks" McDonald's six by fourteen
Billy Gladstone
Midnight Blue pearl/Chrome plating
Wire snares
Author's collection

Stanley Koor's seven by fourteen
Billy Gladstone
Black lacquer/Chrome plating
Gut snares
Author's collection

Four by fourteen Craviatto solid shell Lang Gladstone, Author's collection

Five and one-half by fourteen hand hammered/engraved copper shell Lang Gladstone, Author's collection